APPRENTICESHIP
Embracing Life and Practicing Humanity in the Way of Jesus

Terry B. Kyllo

Published by Hopeful Press, Anacortes, Washington

Contents

*But because being here is much, and because
all this
that's here, so fleeting, seems to require us
and strangely
concerns us. Us, the most fleeting of all.
Just once,
everything, only for once. Once and no more.
And we, too,
once. And never again. Though only once,
having been on the earth—can it ever be
cancelled?*

Rilke
Ninth Elegy, Duino

*I appeal to you therefore, brothers and sisters, by the mercies of God, to
present your bodies as a living sacrifice, holy and acceptable to God, which
is your spiritual worship. Do not be conformed to this world, but be
transformed by the renewing of your minds, so that you may discern what is
the will of God—what is good and acceptable and perfect.*

Romans 12:1-2

Preface

"If your family were better Christians, your mother would not be sick."

I was six years old when a member of Selbu Lutheran Church made this comment to me. Selbu is a small Lutheran congregation near La-crosse, Washington. My mother had been diagnosed with MS one year earlier. I remember the shame I felt at hearing those words. I remember the anger. I remember my panic and confusion as I considered that the Jesus who loved me would hurt my mother because of something bad my family had done.

I wondered if it was true. I wondered what God would do to me if I did something bad. Most of all, I wondered if I was the one who had caused my mother's illness.

A year later, I overheard my father saying that my mom had been fine until I came along, and "that was when her troubles began." That was it then. Without a word, I accepted the blame. Still, I wondered if and how any of it made sense. Would the Jesus who welcomed all the little children make their mothers sick when the children misbehaved?

I now understand that all children will accept the blame for their par-ents' problems. It is easier for them to accept this blame than to accept that life includes such random difficulties. I now understand that my father's words were intended to describe chronology not blame.

I now, too, understand that the woman from Selbu Lutheran was pro-testing both the beauty and vulnerability of life. It was easier for her to as-sign blame than to accept that her life, too, included random difficulties.

For me, the practice of theology has never been an academic exercise. Theology is how I survive, the way I understand and deal with life. Theol-ogy is the practice of careful discernment as we observe what our world-views propose, both on the surface and in their more deeply nuanced underpinnings, and how they form and deform human beings and human community.

Of course, many prefer to remove theology from its art, making of it a law or dictate or one-phrase-fits-all solution to life's problems—like it was used by the woman with her Sunday school smile: as a shield of protection from the hazards of life. She was only one of a vast number of Christians who use theology in this way. Such shields are themselves hazardous, as they separate us from the beauty and joy of life. Those who use theology as a shield are the ones who usually grab the headline news. Yet this, too, offers a clue to understanding the way things are.

My response to this situation is not to abandon the tradition and Scriptures, but to explore them even more deeply. Something in them pointed people toward a new way to live. Something in them proposed a kind of freedom—a risky and responsible freedom—that others have seen and wanted to preserve so that more could hear the proposal and find themselves called by Christ to new life.

I have found myself profoundly disturbed by the difference between the Jesus I see in the Scriptures and the Jesus assumed by the church and by our culture at large. As I've studied the gospel reading each week in preparation for my sermon, I have been challenged. I have been changed.

When I set out on this journey, I did not seek to go where I have been led, now described in the pages of this book; I just wanted to take Jesus seriously and learn to follow him. I have much more to learn.

What follows comes from my journey within community and tradition as I have sought to understand my own life and the life of Jesus. No doubt, the shadows of my early experiences are still present in this work, as they are present in me.

Thanks be to God, the light shines in the darkness!

Introduction

When I was seven years old, a group of boys gathered in front of my house. They had found a BB gun and, spurred on by a boy of 13, were taking turns shooting at birds. I perceived myself to be an outsider to this group. I desperately wanted to be an insider. In an incident I understand much better now, the older boy shoved the gun in my chest and told me to shoot at a bird, concluding with "unless you're chicken." Of course, I was chicken! I was chicken of what all of them would say and think if I did not shoot at a bird. I was terrified, and I can still remember the nauseating ache and sense of disorientation I felt as this fear bored through my gut.

I grabbed the gun. We had seen a robin fly into a hedge, and I figured that if I just stuck the gun barrel into the hedge and fired, I would miss the bird but still be accepted by the group. I could have it both ways. To my great shock and grief, the bird came fluttering out of the bush and flopped on the ground. The older boy then told me I had to "finish off" the bird. He said it was the manly thing to do.

I wept in front of the others, and they laughed. I fled into my house. My gamble to miss the bird and be a part of the group had failed completely. I had shot a bird, and I was a laughingstock.

I wept because I knew what they did not know: Humans and animals are beautiful, and they can break. My mother had been diagnosed with Multiple Sclerosis when I was five years old. I knew that there was enough breaking of animals and humans without our going out to cause more. I wept because I loved robins. I wept because I had gone against my own desires and killed—no, murdered—a fellow creature.

After all the boys had gone, I went outside, took a shovel ,and buried the robin. I could barely look at it.

Why did I do this terrible thing?

This book represents my journey to one understanding of what kind of work is required if we are to avoid succumbing to the human potential for violence, environmental degradation, and despair. I write because I feel compelled to understand the issues myself. I write to better understand myself and the humanity to which I belong.

During the twentieth century, many people gathered together many times and in many places to kill over 260,000,000 people in genocides worldwide. A lot of leadership and organization was required to mobilize those who did the killing, and to immobilize those who were killed. It took effort. Many people were involved in the physical labor required to kill so many people and dispose of their bodies. Most of those involved were not psychopaths, but were, in ordinary circumstances, loving husbands, wives, and parents. Most were ordinary people who did extraordinarily evil things.

We tend to think we would not participate in this kind of evil. Yet in experiment after experiment, 60 to 90 percent of people are willing, sometimes with regret, to inflict pain when an authority figure tells them to do so. Even more disturbing, many of these experiments indicate that our context and the roles we play within that context powerfully shape our actions. Seven year olds are not alone in their willingness to go along with the crowd.

In North America and Europe, we tend to underestimate how strongly culture influences us, yet we know that had we been born in a different culture, we would be very different people. The shared vision for humanity that is culture does not absolutely determine and direct individual action, but it does powerfully shape and direct the potentials that human beings possess. Would most of those who participated in genocide during the last century have killed anyone had they not been ordered to do so?

Western culture has frequently argued about whether nature or nurture has the most sway. Both do. Each tree species has a natural habit of size, branch development, and so on. Yet this natural habit can be trimmed to shape its growth by the art of bonsai. Some have argued that the nurture of culture makes human beings do terrible things, and if we just had more freedom from culture, things would better. Others have said that humans are totally depraved and we must, therefore, increase cultural control to restrain humans. Both of these views miss the point. Human beings are capable of both tender love and vicious violence.

Culture, by creating a set of ideals and stories, trims us and increases the likelihood of certain of our various tendencies. Yet culture itself is one of our capabilities. Culture is itself made possible by our nature and, in turn, shapes the way our nature plays out.

It seems vital then, if we are to address the deep challenges of

- a century of genocide and war,
- how to live with those of different cultures, and
- the human-made but not intended ecological crisis,

we must seek to understand the interplay between culture and human beings.

CHAPTER ONE

Questions on the Way to Hope

We are human. We are capable of wonders. We are capable of deep love. Human, we are also capable of producing and participating in horrors and hatreds that, in one moment, can destroy beauty developed over centuries. Most of us know enough history to have seen myriad negative aspects of human potential and behavior. With these haunting after-images in our minds, it is easy to understand why so many of us feel helpless in our deep uncertainty about the future of human beings and the planet of which we are a part.

Reserve Police Battalion 101

In his book, *Ordinary Men*, Christopher Browning writes about Reserve Police Battalion 101. The battalion was comprised of middle-aged German professional men who were considered too old to go to the front during WWII. They were called together, trained, and sent into villages to round up and kill Jewish residents in occupied Poland. They were not told their specific mission until after they were deployed. Their commanding officer wept as he informed his men of their orders to kill an entire village of Jewish people—men, women, and children. He allowed them to opt out if they objected to the assignment. Browning's research states that 80 to 90 percent of them did not opt out. His explanation of why is chilling:

> Because it was easier for them to shoot. Why? First of all, by breaking ranks, non-shooters were leaving the 'dirty work' to their comrades. . . . It was in effect an asocial act vis-à-vis one's comrades. Those who did not shoot risked isolation, rejection, and ostracism—a very

uncomfortable prospect within the framework of a tight-knit unit stationed abroad.[1]

Why?

The Lucifer Effect

In 1971, 24 Stanford University undergraduates were selected to participate in an experiment led by Philip Zimbardo, a former head of the American Psychiatric Association. The students were divided randomly into "guards" and "prisoners." Zimbardo ended the two-week study after only six days, because those selected to be guards had become alarmingly abusive and many of the "prisoners" had become submissive to the guards' every whim—even to the point of cooperating in abuse of non-conforming prisoners.

In his book, *The Lucifer Effect*, Zimbardo describes what happened to two non-conforming prisoners, numbers "819" and "416," who stood up for themselves against the now dominating guards.

Prisoner 819 tried to remind everyone that this was an experiment and that they did not deserve such brutal treatment. Three days into the experiment, 819 escalated his resistance by not getting out of bed and not eating his breakfast egg. For this, he was placed in solitary confinement. To apply more pressure on him, the prison guards forced his fellow "inmates" to hold their arms out until exhaustion and do meaningless work. Later, the guards made the prisoners repeatedly chant, "Prisoner 819 did a bad thing." Unable to maintain his resistance in the face of both the guards and the prisoners, 819 finally gave in to the "reality" of the experiment. He broke down. Dr. Zimbardo, afraid for 819's mental health, then told him that he was released from the experiment. One would think the student would have been elated to return to his normal world, role, and values. Not so. He wanted to continue and show the others that he could be a good prisoner!

His replacement was prisoner 416, who began a hunger strike after he saw the kind of treatment he and others were receiving at the hands of the guards. He was forced to stay in "the hole" for hours at a time and hold sausages that he refused to eat. As before, the other prisoners were punished for 416's disobedience. The guards set the prisoners against 416 by giving them a choice: They could give up their blankets and 416 could get out of the hole, or they could keep their blankets and 416 could stay in the hole. They chose to keep their blankets and so isolated 416 and rejected his leadership. They, too, wanted to be good prisoners.

Even despite his principled stand against the mistreatment of the prisoners, 416 had lost his ability to realize that he could get out of the prison any time he wanted. When he went to parole board (in yet another part of the experiment), he did not demand that he be allowed to quit the experiment. He could remember that he did not deserve to be mistreated, but he could no longer remember that his was an optional incarceration. His identity had changed because his situation had changed.

Dr. Zimbardo ended the experiment after the guards, using high degrees of verbal abuse, began to force the prisoners into sexual humiliation, grueling numbers of pushups, sleep deprivation, and cleaning toilets with their bare hands—and after a colleague from outside the experiment helped him to see how the experiment was negatively changing Dr. Zimbardo himself.

In a post-experiment interview, Clay (prisoner 416) said that he had begun to lose his identity early in the experiment. While in the experiment, he felt that "Clay" had been put in prison, but he had become "prisoner 416." Clay told one of the guards that he was surprised the guard was capable of treating people in such ways, that he could act this way and not feel, at the time, any guilt for doing so. Another guard said,

> You put on a uniform and you are given a role. I mean, a job, saying 'your job is to keep these people in line,' then you're certainly not the same person if you're in street clothes and in a different role. You really become that person once you put on the khaki uniform, you put on glasses, you take the nightstick, and you act the part. That's your costume and you have to act accordingly when you put it on.[2]

The roles given to each person—whether prison guards, prisoners, or even the staff running the experiment—radically changed their beliefs, values, and behaviors.

Why?

Abu Ghraib

In 2004, U.S. citizens were shocked to learn of the torture of Iraqi citizens by U.S. military personnel at the Abu Ghraib prison in Iraq. The world was stunned by the photos of abuse and degradation, made even more reprehensible by the fact that the photos had been posed with the victims alongside the smiling faces and thumbs-up of U.S. guards. The U.S. was shamed in the eyes of the entire world, yet the U.S. military and Defense Department rushed to defend themselves (and, by extension, the people and government of the U.S.) by dismissing the incidents as the work of a few bad apples. A more careful investigation and analysis revealed that U.S. political and military leaders, dismissing the Geneva Convention, had sent carefully subtle signals to the troops: Take the gloves off to get the information we want. These nuanced signals were powerful, despite long-standing tradition and overwhelming evidence that torture does not produce useful information.

Why did the guards participate in the torture? Why were they smiling in the photos? Why did our leaders attempt to cover up the gloves-off order by scapegoating a few "bad apples?"

Why?

Characteristics in Common

The incidents cited above cannot be dismissed as merely the actions of a few bad apples, as the barrel itself profoundly impacts the apples.

As for Reserve Police Battalion 101, Browning's analysis suggests that any choice to not shoot could have been seen as a moral reproach to the non-shooter's comrades. Additionally, the shooters and non-shooters, alike, portrayed non-shooters as weak and not willing to do their fair share of the work. The courageous choice of 10 to 20 percent not to conform to the orders was seen as a weakness, despite the fact that theirs was the morally superior choice.

These "ordinary men" were not highly indoctrinated SS officers. Most were loving fathers and husbands who went to church, paid their taxes, and loved their country. In their own clothes, many of them would have been considered highly moral, intelligent, and compassionate people. In their own clothes, they would never have thought to kill a Jew or any other person. But when in uniform, the majority of the men of Reserve

Battalion 101 felt that their orders were necessary, justified, and inescapable.

In the Stanford University Experiment, Dr. Zimbardo was careful to select young men who were normal, well-adjusted, and highly intelligent persons. None was prone to violence or criminal behavior. Zimbardo concludes that given clothing, a physical environment, and social pressures, even the most well-adjusted and moral person can quickly lose his or her sense of identity. He goes on to note that, while individuals are responsible for their actions, systems create situations within which the identity of individuals is formed. Further, those who create such systems and situations are also responsible for what takes place in them.

The uniformed men and women involved in the Abu Ghraib tortures were, like the battalion members and university students, quite different people when living their normal roles. Their identities, too, had been re-formed by their situation and its expectations, which allowed them to do things they would never have considered doing under different circumstances and in different clothes.

The Unthinkable Commonality

An estimated 262,000,000 people were killed in genocides worldwide during the twentieth century.[3] It takes a lot of work to kill that many people. Many hands are required. Most of the people who carried out these killings were just like the members of Reserve Police Battalion 101. In the clothes given them by the authorities and in the social context of tight-knit squads, hundreds of thousands of otherwise "good" people killed their first person and then went on killing until nobody else was left to kill.

Moreover, most of those who were to be killed lined up quietly, walked into the woods, lay down, and held tremblingly still until a bullet penetrated their skull. As in the Stanford Experiment, most became "good prisoners" at the hands of their captors and fulfilled their role "well." They submitted, as their role required.

It is not easy for leaders and commanding officers to get people to kill others. It is often estimated that only 40 percent of people in the U.S. infantry ever directly shoot at another person. We do resist killing others, but this resistance can be broken. The story of Reserve Police Battalion 101 (and hundreds of similar stories originating from many different

cultures throughout history) tells us that the vast majority of human beings are capable of pulling the trigger in genocide. You and I are probably
among the vast majority.

Witness Stanley Milligram's famous experiment in which test subjects
were to apply ever-increasing shocks to "help" motivate other people to
answer questions correctly. Sixty-five percent of the test subjects were
found to have administered the highest level of shock—even after in-
dications that the test subjects had passed out or had died! In another
experiment, 21 of 22 nurses were willing to administer double the dosage
of a drug to a patient when told to do so by a doctor, despite the clear
warning against such a dosage on the drug's label.

When asked by an authority to do something unethical or even destructive, the vast majority of us will do it. Seven-year-old boys are not
the only people who can be incited to do what they don't want to do.

Our Response to Social Forces

The enormous power of these social forces to evoke the human potential for dominating or submissive behavior easily leads people to despair
for the future of the human race. Many are led by this despair to retreat
into their homes and hope that such terrible things will not happen in
their backyard.

Such despair is a necessary ingredient for the next genocide, as it creates a hopeless passivity in which even kind and caring people can turn
a blind eye to what would otherwise disturb them into action. For in-
stance, many just do not "know" of the genocide that takes place every
day in our world. Despite an abundance of food, nearly 20,000 people
die each day of starvation, 1.2 billion lack clean drinking water, and 2
billion suffer from micro nutrient malnutrition.

As we look into the future, we hear United Nations' estimates of the
dislocation of 363,000,000 people by 2050 due to global climate change.
Most of those displaced will be from the developing world, which least
contributed to the rise in greenhouse gases that has caused the rise in
global temperature. According to the United Nations 2007-2008 Human
Development Report, the U.S. creates 20.86 percent of the world's CO_2
emissions yet has only 4.55 percent of the world's population. Global
temperature increases of 3° to 4°C could result in 330 million people
being displaced through flooding. Over 70 million people in Bangladesh,

6 million in lower Egypt, and 22 million in Viet Nam could be affected.

Meanwhile, many North Americans go on believing that the key to the ideal human life is to be successful in living the American Dream: having wealth and amassing ever-greater amounts of disposable things. Striving for the contradictory goals of hard work and leisure goods, we now produce 25 percent of the world's emissions of greenhouse gases. We have come to hold consumerism as ideal because we are bombarded by marketing and receive social reinforcement from our friends—along with the threat that if we collectively stopped our consumption, our retirement accounts might crumble.

Like those in Police Reserve Battalion 101, the Stanford Prison Experiment, Abu Ghraib, and a thousand other atrocities, we would act differently in a different social situation, remembering and living out a different set of values. Most of us mean well. Most of us see the beauty of the earth and its people. Most of us want to act responsibly but cannot envision another way to live.

Yet the core issue remains: What is it in us that makes us so susceptible to social forces? And, given the powerful role social forces play in determining our actions, is there any hope for us?

Not the Titanic

On April 10, 1912, the Titanic took off from England to New York on its maiden voyage. After brochures of the ship promoted it as unsinkable, a deck hand was quoted as saying, "Not even God himself could sink this ship."

This belief led the White Star Line to put only one-half of the necessary lifeboats on board and the captain to ignore warnings about large icebergs in his path to New York. They were so secure in their belief in the unsinkability of the Titanic that they could take unnecessary risks and justify their careless behavior. On April 14, they hit an iceberg. The next day, the ship slid into the sea. Only 705 of the 2,200 passengers and crew survived.

We are familiar with this because most of us have seen the movie, *Titanic*. When we watch this movie, we already know the ending. The only drama that remains for us is who will make it to the rescue boats and how well the quartet will play.

Today, many people think that life on earth is like watching a movie about the Titanic. They believe that the earth is the Titanic and that it will soon hit an iceberg and go down. They believe, with the same arrogance of the deck hand, that not even God can save this ship—that is, not even God can save the earth. If this were the case, all we would need to do is sit back, enjoy some good food and champagne, and make sure we have quick access to the lifeboats. We would need to be concerned only with our own and our family's survival and comfort. Any activity directed toward building up the earth in a sustainable way would be like re-arranging deck chairs on the Titanic.

The issues facing us feel so large and complex, while we feel so small and confused. What could we possibly do?

What can we do?

We can do what we can do.

Praying for Our Enemies

In 1997, I became the pastor of a small church in Anacortes, Washington. Before September 11, 2001, I would have considered the congregation able to have difficult conversations and stay together despite differences; I had consciously preached and taught in hopes of strengthening this capacity. Following 9-11, however, this strength and flexibility was greatly diminished as members of our congregation, along with the nation, debated the facts surrounding the events and the reasons, for and against, the U.S. instigating war against Iraq.

The congregation's leaders and I made a decision to get people talking about the possibility of a U.S. invasion of Iraq. We held a series of Sunday events to prepare for this conversation. We were very careful. We did our best to protect the viewpoints of both those for and those against an invasion. We held a potluck, before which people could stand at a microphone and express how they felt. All were encouraged to eat with people who disagreed with their viewpoint. The following Sunday, I preached a sermon highly critical of the administration's use of theology to promote invasion of Iraq, highlighting how theology had historically been subverted to justify, condone, and honor military actions. We were careful to honor the many different perspectives on the Iraq situation as attempts at being faithfully Christian. We were careful not to paint those either pro or anti invasion as good or bad. We remained mindful that all of us were still engaged in grieving the events of 9-11.

Twelve families left the church as the result of those conversations. Many of them did not want to talk to me about their reasons. Many did not seem to know why they had left. They simply could not talk about these issues. It became clear that, for them, the church's job was to support the United States, not to question the wisdom of a public policy decision nor challenge the use of theological language by our elected leaders. Ironically, many of these same people were dismayed by the role the church had played during the Crusades and its use of torture, including water-boarding techniques, during the Inquisition.

In the same vein, I attended a pastors' prayer group in Anacortes for a few months after September 11, 2001. As the U.S. military was initiating its invasion into Afghanistan, pastors offered prayers for the U.S. military and for each administration official by name. They also prayed that George W. Bush would lead the country to a revival—almost as "Pastor-in-Chief," or so it seemed to me. These prayers were affirmed with a breathless "Amen" or "Thank you, Jesus." When my turn came to pray, I prayed for the human beings in the military, for our government to make wise decisions, and for the American people to be bold in speaking their opinions. This prayer brought a few half-hearted "Amens." Then I prayed that all the men, women, and children of Afghanistan would be protected and blessed by God. A cold silence spread over the room.

Afterward, one of the pastors asked me, "How can you pray for our enemies?"

I replied, "Because Jesus tells us to."

"Jesus didn't mean those enemies," he said.

I said that Jesus didn't say we could choose which enemies to love.

He then said that it was important for Christians to obey the governing authorities.

I said that in the United States, "'We, the people, are the governing authorities."

He shook his head.

To my shame, I did not go back to that prayer group. To theirs, they never asked me why I stopped going.

I now understand better why some Christians in my congregation and the pastors in these churches were so unwilling or unable to engage in the self-evident truth that all citizens of this country should question and inform governmental policies. I understand better why these good people were willing to place Jesus at the feet of the born-again George W. Bush instead of asking why he was not doing what Jesus taught.

I was amazed that any disciple of Jesus of Nazareth, who was killed for active yet nonviolent resistance to the Roman Empire, could interpret Jesus' message as simple "support of our country, no matter what."

To understand our capacity for violence, we need to peer as best we can into the heart of our own humanity and consider how social forces work on us. There would seem to be something innate to the human construct that allows social pressures to form our identity and actions so powerfully.

CHAPTER TWO

Humans and Culture

It is a strange thing, being a human. We are alive, yet we know that our life will end. We have such power, yet we know that our powers are limited and often bring unintended consequences. We have the capacity for symbolic thought, memory, reason, and imagination of the future. We know that one day the future will outlast us. This leads us to feel deep inner urgings and longings only hinted at by our words.

The central issue in our experience of being human is that, while we desire life at the core of every cell, we know that we will die. The being that we revel in will one day not be. This conflict between our desire for life and our consciousness of our mortality is inescapable. Ernest Becker called it the "impossible situation" of the human being.

This conflict is key to understanding why humans do what we do.

The clash between our desire for life and our knowledge that one day we will die (whether or not we are always conscious of it) is a relentless daily grind. It calls into question our best work, deepest relationships, and our most joyous occasions. It is the inescapable shadow of our sunniest day. In fact, this conflict threatens us with despair so deep that, like Camus, we might say that there is only one philosophical question: "Why not suicide?"

If we were gods who lived forever, we could deny the terror of our lives. If we were simply animals, we could—oblivious to the fact that the butcher's truck will arrive tomorrow—chew our cud in peace. But we aren't gods and we're not oblivious. We live in the "impossible situation" of being human: We can imagine being god and living forever, but we know that we are not and will not; we will die and must face this fact each moment.

We deny and repress our vulnerability and death, because the reality of our existence terrifies us. In *Denial of Death*, Becker describes the terror we feel at our vulnerability.

> This is the paradox: He [sic] is out of nature and hopelessly in it; he is dual, up in the stars yet housed in a heart-pumping, breath-gasping body that once belonged to a fish and still carries the gill marks to prove it. His body is a material fleshy casing that is alien to him in many ways—strangest and most repugnant way of being that it aches and bleeds and will decay and die. Man is literally split in two: he has an awareness of his own splendid uniqueness in that he sticks out of nature with a towering majesty, and yet he goes back into the ground a few feet in order blindly and dumbly to rot and disappear forever. It is a terrifying dilemma to be in and to have to live with. The lower animals are, of course, spared this painful contradiction, as they lack a symbolic identity and the self-consciousness that goes with it. . . . [Animals] live and disappear with the same thoughtlessness: a few minutes of fear, a few seconds of anguish and it is over. But to live a whole lifetime with the fate of death haunting one's dreams and even the most sun-filled days—that's something else.[4]

Our impossible situation leads to a potentially despair-laden anxiety that threatens to take the joy out of our years. This situation can blind us to the wonder of life, the beauty of the earth, and the pleasure of sun, wind, and rain. How do we escape from this daily grind of consciousness and the anxiety that accompanies it?

To be human is to live a high-voltage existence. The conflict between our desire for life and our consciousness of death creates a lot of charge in us. As human beings became conscious of self, we began to look for ways to adapt to this inescapable conflict. Since we could not resolve the conflict, we looked for a way to insulate ourselves from anxiety and despair, the point at which the voltage of our existence zaps us.

Culture provides this insulation.

This insulation comes in the form of affirmation when we fulfill what culture considers ideal for a human being in our role. (We could also use "meaning" or "purpose," although purpose conveys a more restricted pronouncement). Most of this affirmation comes from within us, as we internalize cultural ideals. We also require affirmation from others. A culture additionally provides ample opportunities for distraction, lots of interesting things to do and much wind to chase. Work, our homes, hobbies, sports teams, shopping, vacations, and recreational opportunities—all afford both affirmation and distraction.

The word "culture" is used in a variety of ways. In this book, culture is the core beliefs, values, and vision shared by a community of people. While culture is manifested in economics, politics, sports, religion, literature, and media, in this book culture describes the beliefs, values, and vision, or "worldview," common to all of these manifestations.

Cultural ideals are expressed in the form of stories or narratives, or, more precisely, in storylines that people within the culture tell over and over again. These narratives powerfully teach and reinforce the beliefs, values, and vision of a culture. They shape our imagination about what is recognized as being ideal for human beings. We hear these stories and strive to fulfill the ideals they illustrate.

Cultures do not tend to deny death itself as a reality, but rather serve to numb us to the emotional and existential consequences of the fact that we all will die and all that we do will turn to dust. We may not be able, as individuals, to stop being vulnerable, but we can fulfill, more or less, what our culture says is ideal. When we are perceived as fulfilling what is considered ideal in our culture we receive its gift: the insulation of affirmation that our lives are meaningful and significant.

Affirmation for having meaning and significance is the gift of culture.

In the face of all that negates human life, culture provides both an ideal for human life and affirmation for those who attain even some part of that ideal. Every day, we hear people make appraisals of others based on these cultural ideals. When we hear something like "She is a good person," these ideals are at work. I have led many funerals as a pastor. Almost without exception, families want me to say "good things" about their deceased loved one. Even when the person who died had been destructive to the family, the family deeply desires that I say something good. What they want to hear me say is that this person fulfilled his or her culturally informed role well.

The religious terms "heaven" and "hell" have at times functioned to label people as being either ultimately ideal or not as described by a culture.

Further, both of these terms carry a (often subconscious) reminder of death. When we are brought to greater awareness of our mortality and limitations, we feel a powerful urge to increase our insulation by defending our culture. We do this by becoming more culturally conventional and protective of our culture as ideal so as to gain the cultural affirmation those stances can provide.

A group of psychologists and sociologist who intuitively agreed with Becker's thesis have developed what they call *Terror Management Theory*. In one of several experiments devised to test this theory (replicated in many cultures), a set of judges was asked to sentence a woman convicted of prostitution. One-half of the group was subtly reminded of death before the sentencing; the other half was not. Those reminded of death required an average of $450 in bond versus an average of $50 required by those who had not been reminded of death.[5] Those who were reminded of their mortality were much more vigorous to defend what they saw as "good" in their society—in this case, by delivering more severe punishment to those whom they felt threatening to the cultural ideal. Terror Management Theory calls this "worldview defense." In the events of September 11, 2001, nearly 3,500 people lost their lives, and the entire U.S. population received a jolting reminder of limitation and death. This increased our propensity for engaging worldview defense with respect to our culture, our nation.

Much of what culture provides human beings is necessary and good. Yet while those in any culture may feel that theirs is eternal and ordained by the gods, culture is not a perfect adaptation to the conflict between our desire for life and our consciousness of death. Culture cannot solve the problem of human existence with any amount of apple pie. Moreover, while culture can help us deal with our mortality and limitation, culture shares both our genius and our fallibility.

Cultures often create social forces that lead people to live in life-destroying ways. As individuals are susceptible to being overcome by bad habits, weaknesses, or over dependence on a single strength, cultures can become victim to their particular form of cultural adaptation to the impossible situation we all face.

The people on Easter Island were great at making boats and warring against one another. But one day, the last tree was harvested, and within a decade or two the last person lay down to die. Rome was great at colonizing and extracting wealth from other lands. After centuries of sending men of marrying age off to fight, the Roman population could no longer provide the troops necessary to maintain their colonies. The Roman Empire fell by the weight of what they considered their success.

We in the Western world are tremendously successful at inventing and using technology. It is so prevalent among us that we do not even question the commonly espoused view that our technology makes us "the most advanced civilization." The by-products of this technology are killing us and depleting our thin blanket of atmosphere. In response to this, we do not consider limiting or regulating our use of technology; rather, we seek a way for more advanced technology to solve the problem. Given the examples of Easter Island and Rome, one wonders if we will do this until the last tree is gone.

Culture Can Be Maladaptive

Culture supplies the human with ways to avoid the constant, grating, emotional awareness of being vulnerable by focusing our attention away from death and limitation and encouraging us to fulfil the cultural ideal so that we can receive its insulating affirmation. While this may help people to live, the anxiety created in us by our no-win situation does not disappear. It goes underground and comes out in strange and unintended ways. It builds up in us, like an electric charge. The ways proposed by culture are often not the best for either the human or humanity as a whole. That is, they can be maladaptive, decreasing the chances for meaningful life now as well as for the future survival of our species.

The ability to form culture is a strength of human beings. Strengths, however, can become weaknesses. Culture shares our limitations and geniuses, and so it can become a nexus for destruction as well as a nest for life. This is what Paul Tillich and others seem to mean by "the demonic": not trouble-making, non-corporeal beings but rather powers and forces that are in themselves good but, in claiming to be ultimate, deform human beings. The patriotism of a people is a good thing. However, blind patriotism—the notion that our culture and country deserve our highest allegiance—is a weapon in the hands of a tyrant.

Nevertheless, we need culture. Expressed in stories, examples, and songs, it provides both compelling distraction and a sense of having others' approval when we fulfill, or as we strive to fulfill, our assigned role.

As Ernest Becker wrote:

> In other words, men [sic] aren't built to be gods, to take in the whole world; they are built like other creatures to take in the piece of ground in front of their noses. Gods can take in the whole of creation because they alone can make sense of it, know what it is about and for. But as soon as a man lifts his nose from the ground and starts sniffing at eternal problems like life and death, the meaning of a rose or a star cluster—then he is in trouble. Most men spare themselves this trouble by keeping their minds on the small problems of their lives just as their society maps these problems out for them. They tranquilize themselves with the trivial—and so they can lead normal lives.[6]

The phrase "tranquilize themselves with the trivial" is a quote from Soren Kierkegaard. Kierkegaard's basic position was that most people are embedded in culture's story of the ideal human without questioning it. Culture functions for them as a painkiller that keeps the terror of life and death at bay, so far repressed that it rarely comes to consciousness as an emotional reality. This painkiller comes with side effects:

- Full Body Cast
- Dangling by the Strings of Culture's Control
- Cultural Blindness
- Destructive Discharge
- Cultural Death
- Wind Chasing
- Violent Response/Scapegoating
- Mortality Guilt and Shame
- Comfortable or Despairing Complacency

Let's explore these briefly now.

Full Body Cast

For those unquestioningly embedded in it, cultural insulation not only insulates from the daily grind of death consciousness but also forms a constrictive shell. This is the first way in which culture can be maladaptive. It can become a full body cast for our individual sense of being human and, collectively, for the way we live out our being as humanity. Here we can imagine being covered in some spray-foam insulation that gets harder over time. The substance of culture's insulation is a mixture of affirmation and distraction. As such, culture not only protects us from our vulnerability but also limits the expression of our unique life as humans and as humanity.

Accepting our culture's notion of the ideal human, we can easily trade some of our freedom for the insulation it provides. We trade away at least some of the possibilities inherent in us. We might be an artist, teacher, or a farmer, but because our culture may not value these occupations, we do something else. Indeed, we are highly motivated to make this bargain with culture when we desperately need the insulation of affirmation and distraction it provides.

Dangling by the Strings of Culture's Control

Being so dependent on the affirmation of culture, we are susceptible to becoming marionettes controlled by those who hold the strings of narrative that sets the culture's sense of the ideal. Unwilling to question our culture and deal with life and death more directly, we place ourselves in dire need of the insulation of culture. Our culture then becomes a company store that provides what we need while inviting us to be ever more deeply indebted to it.

This means that the gift of culture can be used as a means for control when the storylines of culture are left in the hands of authoritarians.

We can become dependent upon the culture to such a degree that we give up our freedom—and even our imagination that we could be free—in return for what culture gives. It takes an act of grace (a free, life-giving gift of affirmation) on the part of God to help us realize that if we have invested our life in a cultural ideal that is not truly ideal, our life still has meaning. It was this grace that caused a former slave trader named Isaac Watts to write "Amazing Grace."

Cultural Blindness

The affirmation we need goes both ways, however. In order to feel the insulation of this affirmation deeply, we need to affirm that our culture is itself ideal or at least superior to any other culture. Because culture insulates us from the high voltage of our impossible situation, we are strongly motivated to ignore or dismiss any information that would undermine our ability to view our culture as an ideal one.

This is the third way culture can be maladaptive: Because we need the insulation so badly, we develop a cultural blindness to the horrors within our culture. This leads to unimaginable suffering and denial that such suffering exists. A citizen whose country exports wholesale violence, degrades the environment, and works trade deals that exploit weaker countries will be strongly motivated not to know what seeds their country is sowing. Knowing would, in effect, be experienced as a death threat. To know would scrape off some of that valuable insulation and open this citizen to the charge of the human desire for life and the reality of death. So many citizens choose not to know, claim their culture's superiority and ignore the very real consequences of unethical behavior on the part of their leaders, government, or corporations. Many Americans believe the U.S. is the most charitable country in the world when, in fact, it is ranked 19th by percentage of GNP according to the Center for Global Development.

Destructive Discharge

Let's use static electricity as a metaphor. Human bodies can build up a static charge. When we shake someone else's hand the electrons in our bodies move to the other person. We feel a part of this shock, but the other person feels it more. Likewise, human beings can build up only so much anxiety before we need to discharge some of it. This leads to the fourth vulnerability of humans and culture: the destructive discharge of this energy to harm others, the world, and ourselves.

Some ways of discharging this energy are healthier than others. Certainly, competing in a basketball game played fairly is a better way to discharge this energy than to duke it out in a bar fight. Other destructive examples include consumerism, drug abuse, work, sex and food addictions, abuse of spouses and children, exploitation of workers, road rage, and self-neglect—to name but a few.

Cultural Death

Some, however, do not or cannot live up to the ideal for a person of their "station." People in this situation experience a kind of cultural death. The poor and the homeless often experience cultural death in the U.S.: They have failed to come anywhere close to achieving the American Dream. They have been so far removed from the ideal that they are considered half-human. Others, simply by virtue of race or gender, are excluded from what culture considers ideal. For example, Africans forced into slave boats were considered three-fifths human. Hispanic migrant farm workers live three-fifths the life span of white Americans. Hitler focused a lot of effort into communicating that Jews, Romani, and disabled people were not really human and needed to be controlled, contained, and, finally, exterminated. Those who are deemed less than culturally ideal become the "disposable people" and are frequently the first objects of hatred when a culture feels threatened. Jesus speaks words of deep hope to the culturally dead of his time—these are the poor in spirit that Jesus called blessed.

Of course, the larger culture—say, that of the United States—is not the only factor we must take into account. Within that culture are many subcultures. Which one matters to us the most is our community of significance: the group of people we look to for our primary sense of affirmation. The subculture of a prison set up by Dr. Zimbardo at Stanford was able to transform normal human beings into dominating guards and submissive prisoners because the culture of their new community of significance said that the ideal guard is "in control" and the ideal prisoner is obedient.

When a culture has too many who are culturally dead, it is in danger of breaking down. Within any culture, subgroups that perceive themselves to be culturally dead often form into groups. Having so grouped, they become powerful subcultures that function for their members in the same way the host culture does for its culturally alive members. Each subculture's codes of honor reveals its understanding of the ideal human. Abiding by the code gives each member the needed insulation he or she was unable to get from the larger culture.

Wind Chasing

Within any larger culture, numerous subcultures give more specific requirements for the human ideal. The young man who tricks out his car with alloy wheels, a spoiler, a flame paint job, and a kickin' sound system is looking for the same affirmation we all seek, only determined by the ideals of his particular community of significance and its culture. Some may think he is ridiculous only because they do not share the subculture of his community. It is the same for the subculture of the über-rich, for whom ownership of museum-quality art displayed on a 420-foot giga-yacht moored off Monte-Carlo is ideal.

The young man and the über-rich have a great deal in common.

Essentially, each is seeking the approval, or the kind of approval that we call envy, from their community in order to gain insulation. The great traditions of the world would say that both of these ways of gaining affirmation are vanity. Nevertheless, all of these examples arise from the same human need: affirmation in the midst of a life that death makes vain.

Mortality Guilt and Shame

When children are faced with a terrible event, they often experience guilt. If their mother or father is killed in an accident, they will most often feel responsible. They do this because they perceive bearing the burden of guilt as better than facing the reality of chance and risk in the world.

In response to my mother's MS, I felt incredible guilt. I felt responsible for her illness and often prayed that God could kill me if she could be well. With my death, the price would be paid and the mistake of my life erased.

Children are not the only ones who tend to embrace a crippling and debilitating guilt rather than accept that the world is unpredictable and sometimes unsafe. This guilt is our fear of mortality and vulnerability shunted into a feeling that promises life will be better if we are "good" from now on.

This could be called mortality guilt. Mortality guilt is an undifferentiated feeling of guilt that is, at its core, anxiety of mortality displaced into a feeling that seems to promise greater control. Mortality guilt is not the same as guilt for having done something wrong (it is appropriate to feel guilty for hurting someone); rather, it is the voltage of human existence expressed without consciously dealing with death and limitation.

Western Christianity has made much of forgiveness of sins. When we have real sins to confess, this is a very good thing. Much of the time, however, it seems that the Western church has set up its rituals to temporarily reduce and manage mortality guilt. When the church did this, it was exploiting human beings rather than teaching them another way to be human.

Additionally, because humans do not feel good about our real situation, we tend toward having deep feelings of shame. Shame is the feeling that there is something intrinsically wrong with us. This is often expressed as shame at our bodies and bodily functions. People often hate their bodies and bodily life, even as they make jokes about such a life. A lot of comedy centers on our experience with bodily existence—jokes about sexual, gastro-intestinal, and other bodily parts and functions. Humans also often deplore the human experience of consciousness being paired with, or arising from and being dependent upon, the body of an animal. As Earnest Becker said, "Humans are gods that shit."

This can lead us to a death wish and rejection of our life-as-it-is. When we resist brushing our teeth or think of committing suicide, we are expressing our deep rejection of our life as an animal who thinks. Unfortunately, Western Christianity has often contributed to the notion that human bodies are shameful and disgusting.

> A priest dies and goes to heaven. He is met by the hospitality committee and is told he can enjoy any of the myriad recreations available. He decides that he wants to read all of the ancient original texts of the Holy Scriptures, and so he spends the next eon or so learning the ancient languages.
>
> After becoming a linguistic master, he sits down in the library and begins to pore over early versions of the Bible. Suddenly, a scream is heard coming from the library.
>
> The angels come running to him, only to find the priest huddled in a chair, crying to himself and muttering, "An 'R'! They left out the 'R'."
>
> God takes him aside, offering comfort and asks him what the problem is.
>
> Through his sobs, he says, "It's the letter 'R'. The word was supposed to be CELEBRATE!"

Cultural institutions and powerful economic and political interests take advantage of the fact that human beings often express the anxiety of our impossible situation through mortality guilt and shame. The Western church, through rituals, allowed people to relieve some of the pressure of mortality guilt and shame without addressing the core issue. This kept people dependent upon the church and therefore easier to control. This falls far short of Jesus' vision for human beings which we will explore later.

Comfortable or Despairing Complacency

Because human beings do not like existence as it is, we wish it were different. But, because we also feel small and vulnerable, we sense the risk involved in working toward a better world. Caught between a desire for change and fear of risk, we vacillate between seeing the world on an inevitable path to progress and seeing it on a hopeless road to destruction. Both of these attitudes lead us to the same response: complacency. We either think our culture will continue to improve without us, so we don't risk ourselves, or we wish our culture was different but aren't willing to face the danger of participating in change or even the challenge of contemplating it. Either way, we remain inert and complacent.

In order to advocate for change, one must be able to 1) question one's own cultural ideals, 2) challenge the cultural ideals of others, and 3) be strong enough and love enough to risk ourselves enough to work for a better world.

Violent Response to Those Who Are Different

Maladaptive culture decreases our chances for long-term survival by fostering violent response to those who are different. We want our cultural narrative to be affirmed so that the affirmation we receive from it is strong. This works well when all we see and know are of our own, same culture. As we become aware of different cultures, however, we feel that our insulation is somehow threatened. (This insulation is, of course, only a construct of our minds.) Feeling weakened by the mere existence of others, we come into contact with our feelings about our impossible situation. Because this situation is truly difficult and terrifying, we often react as if the other group is more of a danger than it is. We will sometimes see the group as, by its existence, the creator of death itself. Hence, we will argue that by killing them, we will kill death, too—at least our awareness of it.

We can see this response in the U.S. after 9-11. U.S. citizens responded so ferociously to Osama bin Ladin not so much because he represented a real threat to each one of us, but because he scratched off some of the interior insulation that keeps us more or less unconscious of death. We responded to him as if he were death itself. We subconsciously hoped that by killing bin Ladin we could destroy death. This response enabled U.S. political leaders to spend trillions of dollars and incur thousands of casualties and injuries to our military personnel to "get bin Ladin." Ironically, most of this effort was not aimed at capturing bin Ladin but in overthrowing Saddam Hussein, who, while he had been quickly linked to bin Ladin, had nothing to do with bin Ladin or with 9-11.

When Osama bin Ladin was killed, many found it difficult to make the distinction between his operational power and the power that we gave him. We can all be happy that his operational power is no more, however limited it was. Yet, as a culture that tries to avoid death, we are in no less danger of being manipulated by those who would use against us our vast pool of anxiety. Bin Ladin certainly took advantage of this. His real power was the power of our own fear. One is forced to wonder if our elected leaders also used the power of our own fear to advance policies they had long held in secret. The key, then, is to do our own work to incorporate our anxiety into our life so that we will be less vulnerable to manipulation by those who would use terror to get their way.

We are not always able to direct our violent response at those who seem responsible for threatening us. This is where humans in culture sometimes engage in scapegoating the weak and vulnerable among us.

Rene Girard proposed this scapegoating process as central to the process of evil. He writes that human beings are different from animals in that we can desire things or roles. Because these things or roles are most often limited in quantity, we rival each other in seeking them. This rivalry can get to the point where it threatens our group or even our whole society. To let off the steam of this rivalry, the rivals unconsciously identify a person or a group of people as the "real source of the problem." They then gain unity and the community is made secure through the purging of emotion on the scapegoat. Later, they may feel that the scapegoat was sent from God to provide this unity. Jesus, Girard says, broke the power of the scapegoating process, because, in his culture, resurrection by God means that he was vindicated as innocent—that is, that Jesus was declared truly ideal after being judged and killed by Roman culture. His resurrection, then, was a powerful reversal: The culture was not ideal, while Jesus was.[7]

I deeply appreciate Girard's work and find it a powerful lens for biblical interpretation and for life in general. However, I feel that he has mistaken the core of the issue, which is not human desire for limited goods, but the fact that humans are themselves limited and mortal. The real issue is the conflict between our drive to live and our consciousness of death, coupled with how we build up powerful charges and then release them on individuals, communities, and cultures.

Deforming Humanity

The men of Reserve Police Battalion 101 (and others who have committed or been complicit in genocide) were willing to do so as a part of a bargain with their culture. In return for their individual freedom, they received insulation from the daily emotional awareness of our impossible situation. Many of them were in the full body cast of their culture's expectations, marionettes to those who controlled the image of the ideal human. In obedience to their culture's ideals, they denied the horrors of their culture. And when affirmation by their culture wasn't enough to fully blind them to the horror, they turned to the numbing effects of alcohol.

They were placed in a situation, given new roles, and indoctrinated to believe that Jews were totally "other," a threat to their families. The only solution was extermination. Their beliefs, values, and vision was powerfully formed by the culture imposed by their government. Their previous beliefs, values, and vision were fairly quickly modified by their Nazi leaders to include and excuse mass murder. Yet this culture, too, offered them the affirmation of meaning and significance when they performed their assigned tasks well. They were given an ideal and affirmation for fulfilling that ideal, and they learned from that ideal to reject those who did not share belief in their mission. Without the ideals of Nazi culture, these men would never have murdered. Without their need for cultural affirmation, they could have more easily refused.

Even so, culture remains a gift. Meaning is central to human life. We do not live by bread alone. We need the affirmation that our lives are worth living. Culture provides the context for meaning and affirmation. How, then, can we receive the gift in a way that lessens its dangers?

CHAPTER THREE

The Teeter-Totter

Cultures fall on a continuum between two vastly different ways of developing this narrative of ideals that we call culture:

1. Denial and Domination – We can deny death and limitation by saying that we are most fully human when we have power over others.
2. Acceptance and Mutuality – We can learn to embrace death and limitation by saying that we are most fully human when we accept our limitation and mortality and as we live in mutual relationship with others.

Denial and Domination Culture

A culture of denial and domination[8] seeks to repress the emotional consequences of death and limitation. It does this by proposing that to be ideally human is to have power—and, of course, we do have power—but since we can't have power in any ultimate sense, we settle for having power over each other in order to fulfill this cultural ideal.[9]

This vision for what it means to be human forms the ultimate apple barrel—that is, the ultimate situation or environment. It sets the tone for a whole people. It is the key social force,

influencing individuals and the structures of human community alike.

We feel pride when we live out the cultural ideal of power. We feel shame when we don't. Living in the ideal of power in a domination culture, we are always over or under someone else. In denial and domination culture, we find ourselves on a never-ending teeter-totter of dominance and submission. When we push off the ground and are "above" another person, we feel the affirmation of fulfilling the ideal of power and status. But only moments later, we realize that we are "below" someone else and feel shame just as intensely.

This teeter-totter dynamic is the beating heart of a domination culture. In this dynamic, we experience the two poles of our existence, one at a time, as if the other does not exist. We feel powerful as if we are not also vulnerable; we feel vulnerable as if we are not also powerful. Up and down, our experience reverses—and with it, our sense of affirmation or shame.

In the second story of creation in Genesis 2 and 3, the woman and man wished to eat the fruit because they wanted to escape human life as God had made it.

> But the serpent said to the woman, 'You will not die; for God knows that when you eat of it your eyes will be opened, and you will be like God, knowing good and evil.' So when the woman saw that the tree was good for food, and that it was a delight to the eyes, and that the tree was to be desired to make one wise, she took of its fruit and ate; and she also gave some to her husband, who was with her, and he ate. Then the eyes of both were opened, and they knew that they were naked; and they sewed fig leaves together and made loincloths for themselves. (Genesis 3:4-7)

The human beings eyes were opened and so they became conscious of their limitation and mortality. Lacking trust in God they "fell" into intense anxiety. Realizing they were naked and vulnerable, the two hid from God because they were afraid. Of course, the story is meant to describe all human beings: At some point, we fall into anxiety about our vulnerability.

God then described some of the key aspects of the result of this fall into anxiety:

> To the woman God said, 'I will greatly increase your
> pangs in childbearing; in pain you shall bring forth chil-
> dren, yet your desire shall be for your husband, and he
> shall rule over you.' (Genesis 3:16)

One important aspect of this story is its description of the teeter-totter of dominance and submission: The man shall rule over the woman. These are the words of a much-saddened God talking about the consequences of their rejection of human life as-it-is. This rejection is played out in domination all the time. The manager dominates an employee, making him feel small and weak. The employee yells at the barista. She goes home and screams at her dog.

These power relationships become enshrined in hierarchies and ranking systems. We seek to climb higher and become more human. We disdain those who are below us as less human or even less than human. We envy those above us and secretly wish they would fall so we could take their place. It is better to be the shooter than to be shot, and so we shoot.

It is important to remember that this is not just the *modus operendum* of the power elites or authoritarian leaders. While a tempting thought, this thought is itself an expression of this very dynamic. Nearly everyone living in a denial and domination culture participates in its power plays; most everyone makes the bargain to avoid the reality of human existence. We buy into the ideal of power and deform our relationships through the teeter-totter of dominance and submission. The energy for this emerges from the central tension between our desire for life and our consciousness of death.

> Authoritarianism is something authoritarian followers
> and authoritarian leaders cook up between themselves.
> It happens when the followers submit too much to the
> leaders, trust them too much, and give them too much
> leeway to do whatever they want—which often is some-
> thing undemocratic, tyrannical and brutal.[10]

Ironically, denying death leads to a culture of death. The impossible ideal of power in denial and domination promotes increased rates of death through violence conducted between humans and violence conducted toward our environment. Being incapable of power over death, we strive for power over others and our environment. Rejecting our own limits, we seek to cross every other limit as well, even when this leads to the destruction of that which supports life.

As a culture trends toward domination, the more brittle the personal "morality" of its citizens becomes. Every culture, even the most domination-based society, has a code of personal conduct that usually includes being nice to people, telling the truth, etc. When power becomes the central the ideal proposed by a culture, however, people are more willing to shed these "morals" in order to attain the culture's deeper ideal.

Human beings living in a domination and denial culture are not the only ones capable of this Dr. Jekyll /Mr. Hyde behavior. Witness the acts of those powerful in the banking, investment, and corporate sector who knew they were endangering the financial system. They "won" by betting on the housing bubble, then on the bust, and then on the bailout. Some have been quoted to say that this was a sign of their intelligence, not an occasion for expressing gratitude to the government of, by, and for the people. I am sure that most of these people are perfectly personable and personally moral.

While denial and domination cultures claim that the ideal human is a powerful one, they do not ignore the fact that humans are also weak. In fact, they exploit our unconscious insecurity as a means to control populations. Domination cultures maintain that the world is dangerous and that only their strong king, ruler, or president can protect their citizens from a bad, violent world.

To keep people dependent on them, leaders (including the media) must spend a lot of time communicating danger to their people. (In recent times, color-coded danger charts were in vogue.) The leader's job is to subdue chaos and keep us safe. Such leaders must tell us that a lot of chaos exists and they need extraordinary powers to combat it—albeit, the leader rarely leads the charge. Ironically, to protect us from a dangerous world, the extraordinary powers we grant to the leader include authority to send thousands or millions of our fellow citizens to death in battle.

Even the lowliest person in the pyramid of human worth can rejoice, however, when their nation, tribe, or basketball team wins the battle. Then, everyone gets to feel powerful vicariously: "I may be the lowest of the low, but it's better to be me than the king who got defeated." The boy who worked the bellows for a helmet manufacturer in the outskirts of Rome and was daily beaten by his master felt the rush of power whenever the Roman legions claimed yet another territory and sent praise to Nike, the goddess of victory. Chaos had been defeated again, and his culture was again shown to be ideal because it had "won."

Denial and domination cultures celebrate violence as the way to salvation. If life is a power contest for dominance, then violence is necessary and even good. Walter Wink has written brilliantly about how our entire culture sees violence as salvation. Everything from Popeye the Sailor Man to movies, TV shows, and even the U.S. national anthem's "bombs bursting in air" suggests that when the chips are down, the only way to safety is to win at violence.

For a leader of a domination society, it is not too difficult to move people toward violence. This is accomplished by exploiting both our need to be powerful and our fear of being vulnerable.

> Of course the people don't want war. But after all, it's the leaders of the country who determine the policy, and it's always a simple matter to drag the people along whether it's a democracy, a fascist dictatorship, or a parliament, or a communist dictatorship. Voice or no voice, the people can always be brought to the bidding of the leaders. That is easy. All you have to do is tell them they are being attacked, and denounce the pacifists for lack of patriotism, and exposing the country to greater danger. (Nazi leader Hermann Goering)

The reality is that we humans are both strong and weak. Both are true of us all of the time. In denial and domination cultures, however, we imagine that we are either one or the other. Humans in domination culture do not hold the two together in one reality very well. All the leaders have to do is say that our culture is being threatened and a rush of anxiety washes over us as if we have no power at all. Not liking this anxiety at all, we soon wish to exterminate those who, we are told, threaten our existence. We rush to dominate them and give our leaders power to protect us by sending us to war.

Acceptance and Mutuality Culture

It is interesting to note that whenever I show the pyramidal illustration of denial and domination culture, almost everyone says that this is the reality they experience. Few are able to offer an alternative drawing about how human community can be organized. This is shocking in a country founded with the words "We the People."

Despite our lack of imagination about what it might look like, we sense there is another way. This other way could be described as a culture of acceptance[11] and mutuality. Instead of denying the daily emotional impact of death and limitation, the ideal human in this culture learns to embrace our situation. The ideal human learns to embrace the reality that we are strong and weak, alive and mortal, powerful and vulnerable—and that we are all of these things in every moment of our existence. The ideal human is one who learns that everyone is in the same boat. We are one human family living in the same situation. All are God's children and all fall short of the glory of God.

As we relate to one another in a culture of acceptance and mutuality, the ideal human seeks neither to gain dominance nor to fall into submission, but to strive to better relate to all others as equals. We learn to resist the dynamic of the teeter-totter of dominance and submission. We remember we are both powerful and vulnerable—both, at all times.

Again, culture as the central vision for what it means to be human powerfully forms the ultimate situation or environment of human beings and human community. The worldview or cultural ideal of mutuality creates a totally different set of social forces than a domination culture. A mutuality culture therefore organizes in a more circular fashion.

The Jewish and Christian movements began as attempts to create a mutuality culture in the midst of a culture of domination. In Philippians, Paul quotes what may have been an early creed or a part of a liturgy in the early church:

> Let the same mind be in you that was in Christ Jesus, who, though he was in the form of God, did not regard equality with God as something to be exploited, but emptied himself, taking the form of a slave, being

> born in human likeness. And being found in human
> form, he humbled himself and became obedient to the
> point of death—even death on a cross. Therefore God
> also highly exalted him and gave him the name that is
> above every name, so that at the name of Jesus every
> knee should bend, in heaven and on earth and under
> the earth, and every tongue should confess that Jesus
> Christ is Lord, to the glory of God the Father. (Philip-
> pians 2:1-11)

This passage is an attempt to redefine the notion of the ideal human
from that promoted by the Roman ideal of denial and domination to one
befitting a culture of acceptance and mutuality. This early church creed
or hymn claims that the true character of God, and therefore the true
character of human beings and human community, is life giving service
and mutual relationship. It suggests that the only lord worth bending the
knee to is not Caesar with his armies, but Jesus—whose suffering love on
behalf of the whole world led him to the cross.

When we see Jesus on the cross, we see the true nature of God.

This suffering love is what God exalts because it reflects God's values
and the way God intends humans and human community to behave.

> Awe came upon everyone, because many wonders and
> signs were being done by the apostles. All who believed
> were together and had all things in common; they would
> sell their possessions and goods and distribute the pro-
> ceeds to all, as any had need. Day by day, as they spent
> much time together in the temple, they broke bread at
> home and ate their food with glad and generous hearts,
> praising God and having the goodwill of all the people.
> And day by day the Lord added to their number those
> who were being saved. (Acts 2:43-47)

The early Christian communities are examples of mutuality culture.
Jesus' main term for this was "the kingdom of God": the sphere of God's
influence. One could express this as God's Reign of Mutuality. In Acts
2, early Christians gave up possessions and shared with each other so
that all had enough to eat and so that the most vulnerable in society
(domination cultures create lots of these) were also given enough to eat.
Rodney Stark, a historian at the University of Washington, theorizes that
the Early church grew in part because it valued caring for those made

vulnerable by the Roman domination system.[12]

As Reinhold Niebuhr pointed out is his book, *The Nature and Destiny of Man,* love is more difficult when attempted in or between larger groups of people. He argued that individuals and small groups are more able to love in a sacrificial way than are larger groups. He is right, and his view is widely held by many—including President Barac Obama, who says he is a disciple of Niebuhr. The larger the group, the more the group will need to rely on process to help balance the needs of the many, the needs of the one, and the long-term consequences of meeting these needs. All too often, however, Niebuhr's point of view can be interpreted so as to underestimate the effect of a culture's ideal on its citizens and how carefully leaders must cultivate this ideal. Unfortunately, politicians have used Niebuhr's view as their excuse when claiming they have done all they can to promote mutuality, when this has clearly not been the case. In this way, Niebuhr's view has become a lot like Augustine's Just War Theory—instead of being rigorously applied, it is used as cover.

A culture of mutuality encourages its citizens toward conscious awareness of how culture can become maladaptive, and then seeks to decrease these tendencies. A culture of mutuality encourages an attitude of respectful and playful questioning of power and its uses. It encourages its citizens to actively participate in local democratic processes. It fosters an environment in which the vulnerable are protected. It seeks to level the playing field between the rich and the poor so that every voice is heard. It seeks to hold the tension between the rights of the majority and the rights of minorities. It handles conflict by talking and reasoning. This sort of thing was in the mind of the founders of the U.S. as they sought to separate the powers of the king into three separate branches of government, installed an inheritance tax to keep a wealthy elite from forming, made war more difficult to wage by requiring legislative approval, and established a bill of rights to protect individuals and groups from the tyranny of the majority.

Sin

Given the fact that almost any of us would prefer a mutuality culture to a domination culture, why is it that human beings so often form into domination cultures?

There is no easy way to say this: Human beings often lack the courage to embrace an existence that includes life and mortality, our power and vulnerability. We choose to make our lives small and surrender our as yet unknown potential as a vulnerable and powerful human for a prerecorded, culturally insulated life.

As persons, sin is a gut-level rejection of life-as-it-is to avoid our fear of life that includes death. Sin is the narrowing of our human experience to avoid the death and limitation that are woven into it.

In our highly individualistic culture, we are used to speaking of "sin" as a term that applies to individuals. In the scriptures, however, sin also applies to the People of Israel's missing the mark of mutuality culture. Sin is often a description of domination culture. The relational teeter-totter of domination culture is a result of our rejection of life-as-it-is. We try to be either God or less than human because being human—that is, being human with its contradiction and conflict—is too painful and terrifying. In domination culture, we are endlessly being either dominant or submissive to one another.

Luther called theology that supported the ideal of power a "theology of glory."

> A theologian of glory calls evil good and good evil. A theologian of the cross calls the thing what it actually is. This is clear: He who does not know Christ does not know God hidden in suffering. Therefore he prefers works to suffering, glow to the cross, strength to weakness, wisdom to folly, and, in general, good to evil. . . . God can be found only in suffering and the cross, as has already been said.[13]

The ideal of power is always pointing a finger at the weakness of the one suffering and saying, "If you were really worthwhile, you would have power yourself." The ideal of power invalidates us all, as we are all vulnerable and mortal as well as capable and alive. Our mortal flesh, even with our best intentions and on our best day, is crushed under the weight of this illusion. Of course, this invalidation of human beings serves to benefit the powerful. A powerless populace is often willing to make more bricks with less straw rather than experience the risky freedom of the wilderness.

A theologian of glory is one who is so captivated by the ideal of power that he or she cannot see the destruction waged by such a worldview. A theologian of glory actually supports domination and serves as its priest.

Thomas Merton resonated with this perspective in his journey towards freedom. Despite its crushing weight, we continue to be attracted to the siren call of denial and domination culture, which he calls "the world."

> We must be saved from immersion in the sea of lies and passions which is called "the world." And we must be saved above all from the abyss of confusion and absurdity which is our own worldly self. The person must be rescued from the individual. The free son of god must be saved from the conformist slave of fantasy, passion, and convention. The creative and inner self must be delivered from the wasteful, hedonistic, and destructive ego that seeks only to cover itself with disguises.[14]

Of the two courses available (denial or embrace of life-as-it-is), we often choose the one that most helps us deny our mortality, thereby affording us the illusion that we won't die. We choose denial and buy into futile power games, hoping we will come out on top. But this is truly vanity, as even Augustus Caesar found out on his deathbed. The pharaohs' tombs have become dust. We participate in the degradation of the environment, sell people, enact the illusion of power, and destroy the future for our grandchildren. We destroy or diminish the earth and one another and our own selves for the insulation of denial and domination—and, in the end, all this that we have done amounts to nothing.

This is why humans are so willing to make a bargain with a domination culture: It provides us with the insulation of meaning and affirmation of our existence without our having to engage death. In return, we take on the culturally defined roles that are available to us. Given a different culture, might not the yachting couple find enjoyment in choosing to pay their workers more or create sustainable agriculture for a whole region in Africa with the cost of the yacht? Given a culture of mutuality, might not the young man have chosen to find a deeper affirmation in fixing the car of an elderly woman rather than adding a flame job to his own. Each of us might make similar choices, but do we?

This is true of a whole people as well as individuals. If everyone had had imaginative freedom in Pharaoh's Egypt, the populace might well not have chosen to build pyramids for one soon to be dead human. They might have used that energy to build parks where families could walk and play. The Roman people might well have chosen to live more simply and not send their men away from home to kill and die on others' soil. They, too, might have enjoyed a few more sunsets with their families and found meaning in less destructive ways.

I have been in the room before and during the deaths of some extremely "successful" people. In the days and hours leading to their death, many of them have confessed that they had placed their wealth above their families. Some have gone so far as to say that the competitive drive for money had ruled their lives. Searching for the affirmation through wealth, power, and the respect or envy of their peers they lost sight of their family. On their last bed, they were forced to wonder if it had been worth it. One man wept when his daughter arrived, knowing that his estranged son would not. After a tearful phone call in which the man apologized for being absent to his children, his son arrived for his last hour. The healing began. That was good, but the wounds were great.

Christianity began as Jesus worked to free people from the bargain we make with denial and domination. He sought to return to us our birthright as human beings: the perilous freedom and responsibility of love that is God's gift to us.

Jesus invites us to do our own, deep, spiritual work to bring our anxiety about life-as-it-is in consciousness so that we will be less vulnerable to manipulation by those who would use terror to get their way. He invites us to do this deep work so that we can join him in leading others toward a more full expression of God's Reign of Mutuality.

In the movie, *The Matrix*, Neo is freed from the control of machines that use human beings as a source of power. While being used as a power source, millions of human beings were living in a computer-generated dream world that kept them from conscious awareness of their slavery. The movie eventually reveals that each person subconsciously knows the truth and could choose to get out, yet they choose to not leave because the real world is more terrifying than the dream world created for them by the machines. This movie has held a deep resonance for its audience in the last decade, not only because its story became a metaphor for the corporate influence on our modern lives but also because we know that we, too, are enslaved and constricted by a culture that is trending toward domination.

Some of us want out and hope that Morpheus will find us.

Another Way

Human beings have another option for how we can respond both to our impossible situation and the denial and domination cultures within which we live. If we were to learn to embrace our situation more consciously, we might well need less cultural insulation. If we could learn to do this, we might find ourselves in a stronger bargaining position with culture. We might not settle for being a stonemason when poetry is our true calling, or vice versa. We might not settle for a culture that enslaves people or degrades the environment. We might not settle for killing our human brothers and sisters, degrading our environment, or abusing prisoners. We might not settle for just going along with the crowd should the nation cheer a war of whim. We might not pull a trigger in order to live up to an cultural ideal in a moment that we will regret for the rest of our days.

In his brilliant book, *Courage to Be*, Paul Tillich speaks of both the "courage of despair" and "the courage to be." What he seems to mean is that it takes courage to consciously acknowledge death as a part of life and courage to go on living in the face of that reality. To do this, we must, according to Tillich, "be grasped by the God beyond our idea of God." Being held in this way, in the midst of our anxiety, provides for us what Tillich calls "absolute faith." By this, he does not mean *absolutist* faith, but a deep movement in which we experience courage to embrace both life and death and to say "yes" to a life that includes both.[15]

In elementary and junior high school, I was bullied a lot, yet I often had some capacity to resist the bullies. I had this capacity because I had come into a powerful awareness of my mortality through the illness of my mother. This did not make me free, however. It meant that I needed to "be a good boy" more than most children did. They could play fast and loose, because they were blissfully unaware of human vulnerability and death. Whereas they had not yet touched the high-voltage lines, I had, and I felt I needed all the insulation from future jolts that I could get. I needed to live up to the highest ideals I could find. When I didn't, I felt terrible guilt and shame.

On the other hand, awareness of mortality did give me the ability to question my classmates' notion of the ideal: to be powerful. I decided that the ideal of power was a lie, and so I was led to the next question: What ideal might make life worth living? This initiated my journey into theology, the critique of how cultures form and deform human beings.

After I killed and buried the bird (if you missed it, see page 4), I felt terrible for days. Without having the words to state it, I decided then that I would not go along with others when I didn't want to. Trading my humanity for entrance into the cool kids' group was not worth the inner pain. There had to be another way.

Blindsight

The men of Battalion 101 committed atrocities in the name of Hitler's ideal. For most of them, their actions increased their dependence upon their culture and diminished their ability to question its ideals as truly ideal, resulting in blind allegiance. The Nazis counted on this tendency and referred to it as *blutkitt* (blood cement).

The more we have sacrificed our authenticity to fulfill our cultural ideal, the more strongly we are motivated to affirm our culture as truly ideal. Paradoxically, this means that groups participating in genocide will more fervently believe in the superiority of their culture than will the rest of us.

This is the reason why so many U.S. citizens do not feel it important to acknowledge (let alone accept responsibility) that an estimated 1,000,000 Iraqis have died in the Iraq war, and 2.5 million have become refugees. This is also why most in the U.S. turn a blind eye to the thousands of Iraqi refugee children forced into child prostitution in Syria.[16] This is why we, as a nation, resist delving into incidents of U.S. perpetrated or sanctioned torture and assigning responsibility; instead, we would rather debate which forms of cruelty and dehumanization fall under the definition of torture—in essence, hoping to remake Guantanamo by changing its name to Geneva. We need to discount such information because we don't want to diminish the culture whose affirmation we need in order to handle our life. It is also for this reason that many American Christians so fervently insist that the role of their faith is to support their country, no matter what. Jesus is the embodiment of the ultimate ideal for Christians, and since we need our country and culture to be ideal, we need Jesus to bless it.

To summarize: The situation human beings face is truly and extremely difficult to deal with. The cost of dealing consciously with it is high, and many choose the broad and easy path that leads to destruction (denial and domination). We tend to develop domination cultures because we don't want to take the narrow path of claiming courage in the face of our mortality and limitation. This increases the likelihood of our becoming vulnerable to the ways culture can be maladaptive and decrease our chances of survival.

Embracing Our Shadow

Nevertheless, it is possible for human beings to embrace our situation and live out more concretely a culture of mutuality. Ursula K. Leguine wrote about this possibility in her acclaimed *EarthSea Trilogy*. As a young wizard, Ged plays with powers too great for him to control, and he sets free a terrible shadow on the world. Later, he confronts the shadow that has haunted and hunted him. Finding his enemy, the shadow of his own death, he embraces it and is made whole. In the third book of the series, Ged, along with a young prince named Arren, sets out on a quest to heal a rift in the world and the human heart that had been created by a man who sought immortality and was draining the world of joy and health.

> **Arren**: Where are the servants of this—Anti-King?
> **Ged**: In our minds, lad. In our minds. The traitor, the self; the self that cries I want to live; let the world burn as long as I can live! The little traitor soul in us, in the dark, like the worm in the apple. He talks to all of us. But only some understand him. The wizards and sorcerers. The singers; the makers. And the heroes, the ones who seek to be themselves. To be oneself is a rare thing and a great one. To be oneself forever: is that not better still?
> **Arren**: You would say to me that it is not better. But tell me why. I was a child when I began this voyage, a child who did not believe in death. You think me a child still, but I have learnt something, not much, maybe, but something: I have learnt that death exists and that I am to die. But I have not learnt to rejoice in the knowledge, to welcome my death or yours. If I love life, shall I not hate the end of it? Why should I not desire immortality?
> **Ged**: Why should you not desire immortality? How should you not? Every soul desires it, and its health is in the strength of its desire—But be careful; you are one

who could achieve your desire.

Arren: And then?

Ged: And then this: a false king ruling, the arts of man forgotten, the singer tongueless, the eye blind. This! —this blot and plague on the lands, the sore we seek to heal. There are two, Arren, two that make one: the world and the shadow, the light and the dark. The two poles of the Balance. Life rises out of death, death rises out of life; in being opposite they yearn for each other, they give birth to each other and are forever reborn. And with them all is reborn, the flower of the apple tree, the light of the stars. In life is death. In death is rebirth. What then is life without death? Life unchanging, everlasting, eternal?—What is it but death—death without rebirth.[17]

The hope for a culture of mutuality and a new way to handle our fear of death are at the heart of authentic Judaism and Christianity, despite the fact that this heart has often been encased in the cross-embossed armor of Empire.

CHAPTER FOUR

Jesus' Radical Proposal

Jesus of Nazareth made a radical proposal to his apprentices about how individual humans can live with one another and be humanity. The word "radical" comes from the Latin word radix, which means "root." Jesus made a proposal for life that recognized the root of our humanity.

Jesus was a radical human. He taught us to embrace human life as it truly is.

Jesus was a radical human. He taught us how to participate in God's vision of humanity.

Central to his teaching about how to be human is baptismal awareness. He taught this with every action and statement. He explicitly expresses it in Luke:

> Then he said to them all, 'If any want to become my followers, let them deny themselves and take up their cross daily and follow me. (Luke 9:23)

The Empire's Cross

Let's be clear: Nobody in the first century ever took up a cross more than once. Historians tell us that the Persians likely invented crucifixion between 300-400 BCE as a way to intimidate masses of people into submission. Crucifixion brought together not only the normal fear of pain, torture, and death that all of us share but also the fear of being naked, humiliated, and killed without a burial—especially abhorrent in Middle Eastern culture. In fact, to see the nakedness of another was shaming to the viewer. Crucifixion was intended to shame and intimidate the whole population.

In the Roman Empire, crucifixion was a punishment for non-citizens engaged in rebellion. It was used against the bandits, zealots, and terrorists of Jesus' day. Crucifixion provided a rich canvas of tortures from which the executioner could choose. The site was carefully chosen to be highly visible to the population, perhaps along the major roadways into town, to maximize the effect of its terror. There, crosses were filled with the dying and the dead. Birds, rats, and insects were there too, attracted by the odors of blood, death, and decay. A sign describing the crime was customarily hung around the neck of the accused, who carried the horizontal portion of the cross to a pole that had been left in the ground from the last crucifixion. No doubt, bones, stench, and human excrement surrounded the pole, signs of a previous victim.

The victim was stripped, then flogged with a flail of iron balls and sharp bits of bone or metal. Every movement and moment of the victim was painful after that. At the crucifixion site, the wrists of the victim were tied and nailed to the cross beam before the victim was raised up on the pole. Finally, the feet or ankles were nailed to the pole. Death usually came after several days of blood loss, exposure, thirst, trauma, and strangulation by the muscles of the chest being torn from the rib cage and constricting airflow in the neck. The body was left hanging for all to see as a terrible reminder of the possibility of crucifixion for them should they step out of line. Years of movies and mass-produced cross necklaces have made us numb to the function and meaning of the cross in Jesus' day.

What did Jesus mean, then, when he said that to be his apprentice means to take up our cross daily and follow him?

Baptismal Awareness

First, Jesus is leading us to a new way to be human. Jesus' invitation to take up our cross daily means he is inviting us to engage our impossible situation consciously in spiritual practice. Instead of repressing and denying the emotional consequences of our power and vulnerability, life and mortality, he asks us to embrace our true situation. He asks us not to give up or restrict life in order to avoid our anxiety about death by encasing ourselves in the insulation of culture. He asks us to engage the high voltage of human existence so that it does not build up so much charge in us. As Dietrich Bonhoeffer wrote: "When Christ calls a man [sic], he bids him die."[18]

Gandhi wrote something similar as he reflected on the spiritual work he needed to do in preparation for his nonviolent leadership:

> I have deliberately made a supreme attempt to cast out from my heart all fear whatsoever, including the fear of death. Still, I remember occasions in my life when I have not rejoiced at the thought of approaching death as one might rejoice at the prospect of meeting a long-lost friend. Thus man [sic] often remains weak, notwithstanding all his efforts to be strong, and knowledge which stops at the head and does not penetrate into the heart is of but little use in the critical times of living experience.[19]

The effect of this is akin to what people experience when they learn they have only one year to live. People in this situation frequently experience both grief and renewed vitality. They tend to take less seriously the often unspoken expectations of family and friends to conform to culture's demands. During this time, enhanced grief is accompanied by a more joyous and liberated life, and their newfound awareness of their death leads to freedom.

Facing death every day is central to what Martin Luther called a theology of the cross. In the following quote, he talks about the Christian baptism as not a once-and-done ritual but rather a daily experience.

> He, however, who has been emptied [Cf. Phil. 2:7] through suffering no longer does works but knows that God works and does all things in him. For this reason, whether man [sic] does works or not, it is all the same to him. He neither boasts if he does good works, nor is he disturbed if God does not do good works through him. He knows that it is sufficient if he suffers and is brought low by the cross in order to be annihilated all the more. It is this that Christ says in John 3[:7], "You must be born anew." To be born anew, one must consequently first die and then be raised up with the Son of Man. *To die, I say, means to feel death at hand.*[20] [emphasis mine]

Christian baptism, then, is not a required payment for a ticket to heaven, nor is it just another way to be affirmed by culture; it is an invitation to a new way of being human that embraces our humanity.

> To be a Christian does not mean to be religious in a
> particular way . . . but to be a human—not a type of
> human, but the human God creates in us.[21]

Baptism is a rite of entry into the community of Jesus' apprentices. In early Christianity, it marked a change from one worldview to another, from allegiance to Caesar to allegiance to Jesus. In baptism we are invited to embrace the reality of death in life and find ourselves emptied of what Luther called works—that is, trying to be ideal in the eyes of our culture and being bound by them. Because we have been grasped, as Tillich wrote, by the God beyond our idea of God, we have the courage to embrace a life that includes life and death and find a new freedom. This is perhaps what Martin Luther had in mind when he wrote, "The Christian is a perfectly free lord of all, subject to none; the Christian is a perfectly dutiful servant of all, subject to all."

Jesus is leading us to see that these two belong together: Conscious and heartfelt grief for the reality of death is a necessary part of a vibrant life. This is what I mean by baptismal awareness. Many theologians and writers of biblical texts have used the term daily baptism. This conjures an image of a once-a-day reminder. As such, this term falls short, I think, of their intention. Expressed as baptismal awareness, I am suggesting a moment-by-moment consciousness of embracing life-as-it-is.

This is what Jesus means when he says that he "came that we might have life abundantly." Denial takes energy, and lots of it. When we don't face our true situation as human beings, our latent anxiety forms an undertow in our lives; when we take on this anxiety more consciously in daily spiritual practice, we find ourselves freer the rest of the day. We are able to tap into and utilize a new source of energy—not only because we no longer need to expend a massive amount of energy in order to keep up our denial but also because we now know that each moment is a precious gift of God.

> Come to me, all you that are weary and are carrying
> heavy burdens, and I will give you rest. Take my yoke
> upon you, and learn from me; for I am gentle and hum-
> ble in heart, and you will find rest for your souls. For my
> yoke is easy, and my burden is light. (Matthew 11:28-30)

In baptismal awareness, we live a more abundant life because we have shed the heavy yoke of domination culture. We are able to recognize and lift the burden of our cultural insulation and its constrictive shell. We begin to discern beliefs, vision, and values that are authentic and life-giving.

Contemplating the Blessing

Here, we need to step back for a moment. There are people who have experienced so much of life's pain in war, abuse, violence, and economic deprivation that they do not need so much to contemplate their vulnerability as their legitimate and God-given power. People having these experiences may need to contemplate the goodness of existence; the wonder of creation; comfort and laughter in community; and, in their practice of baptismal awareness, the still small voice of God on the mountaintop.

Indeed, it would be possible to read this book and let our imagination shift from the temptation of denial of our death and vulnerability to a manic focus on them. While we may benefit from some such focus for a season, we must recognize the temptation to see life as devoid of goodness. This would be just another expression of rejecting of life-as-it-is. It is one I have sometimes been susceptible to—due, perhaps, to both my northern European ancestry and my early childhood experiences.

Jesus invites us to see that our life as creatures, which includes vulnerability and death, is good and affirmed by God. Some may need to spend more time working towards consciousness of death, while others may benefit from spending more time in awareness of the goodness of life and creation. We may go through seasons in which we need to shift from one to the other, or even hold them consciously together.

Cyprian, a Bishop in Carthage, in the midst of the domination culture of Rome, told new baptismal candidates that baptism was their entrance back into the earth as paradise. He reminded them of God's blessing of their life. Could it be that with such a blessing he was not denying death and vulnerability, but that his congregations needed to hear about the beauty of the earth because death and vulnerability were so obvious?[22]

It is important to realize that such a blessing as Cyprian gave can also be painful. In my years working in the Episcopal Church, I have learned to appreciate more deeply the gift of blessing. Episcopalians are very good at it. It would be naïve to think that such blessing is easily accepted, and equally naïve to think that it is only comfort food. Such a blessing can help us face the resistance we feel to life-as-it-is and learn to embrace that life better. A word of warning, however, seems necessary: It is possible to bless people in such a way that pain, suffering, and death are denied as parts of life. This is the blessing of Disneyland people in a make-believe world and is no blessing at all. The blessing of Jesus both acknowledges and leads us to consciousness of the true condition of the human experience and to its embrace.

Reign of Mutuality

The effect of Jesus' profound proposal can now be stated simply: As we learn to embrace our situation, we need less of the insulation culture provides. We shed some of this insulation and find ourselves less constricted. We need smaller doses of the "tranquilizer of the trivial." We are freer to discover and be who we are.

This leads to a second meaning of his invitation: As we need less of the affirmation culture provides, we gain freedom from its constricting layer of insulation and can see our culture more for what it is and how far short of the ideal of a mutuality culture it is.

Since we no longer need culture so badly and so blindly, we can question what kind culture we are living in and what kind of culture might be better. This is not to say that we lose all need for culture or can be freed from needing a proposal for the ideal human. Culture itself is not the problem. Its immense power, however, can be abused by those with authoritarian leanings, either as dominant or submissive authoritarians. Culture can be a blessing when, together, we strive for mutuality.

Jesus proposed an ideal that includes embracing our condition and enacting love for all our neighbors. He proposed that we strive for what Ernest Becker called a "cosmic ideal," rather than merely the ideal we might receive from our own culture.

Jesus sought to teach us how to embrace life and death, our power and our limitation. This baptismal awareness leads toward greater freedom from our cultural insulation so that we might begin living with one another in the Reign of God. Jesus interweaves these two themes as necessary parts of one another throughout his teaching: 1) embracing our condition (our vulnerability as part of the goodness of life) through baptismal awareness and (2) engaging in nonviolent public leadership that moves us from domination to mutuality.

The gospel writers summarized this cosmic ideal using the term "kingdom of God." There are many ways to translate this important term: reign of God, community of God, reign of love, collaboration of God, kin-dom of God, environment of God, economics of God, the vulnerability of God, culture of God, or government of God. The idea of the kingdom of God is the sphere of influence of God. Of the many good attempts to describe the tantalizingly difficult concept of the Reign of God, I wish to use "God's Reign of Mutuality."

> A dispute also arose among them as to which one of them was to be regarded as the greatest. But he said to them, 'The kings of the Gentiles lord it over them; and those in authority over them are called benefactors. But not so with you; rather the greatest among you must become like the youngest, and the leader like one who serves. For who is greater, the one who is at the table or the one who serves? Is it not the one at the table? But I am among you as one who serves". (Luke 22:24-27)

We often underestimate the importance of this passage. Here, Jesus critiques the heart of Roman culture as a domination culture, a culture in which leaders "lord it over them." Roman culture, as experienced both individually and communally, was fully in the grasp of the teeter-totter of dominance and submission. Jesus proposes that God envisions the central dynamic of humanity as one of mutual vulnerability and power. He calls his apprentices to a community in which status, age, and position are replaced by mutual service and relationship through awareness that all are in the same boat and that this boat is good.

God's Reign of Mutuality is at the core of Jesus' teachings on how to be humanity.

Mutuality in the Midst of Empire

Jesus called apprentices who would engage and continue to practice baptismal awareness, along with both inward and outward focused participation in God's Reign of Mutuality. He called his apprentices to be nonviolent public leaders in God's ongoing healing of the world.

In our time, the term "disciple of Jesus" is nearly broken, seeming to refer to one who merely believes certain things or who has had a religious experience of Jesus that entitles him or her to Jesus' religious services. I use the word "apprentice" to correct this passive notion of discipleship.

Apprenticeship involves a process of learning from an advanced practitioner of a particular discipline the art, craft, and skillful use of the tools required to successfully engage in the work of that discipline. Jesus sought, and was sought by, apprentices who would come to share his values, beliefs, and vision and who would learn from him the skills to live this vision in the midst of empire, transforming it from within.

The Gospels are quite clear that Jesus did not intend his disciples to passively receive his religious services, but desired them to practice both his way of being human and his form of leadership within the larger culture. Jesus continues to summon apprentices.

Jesus' invitation to take up the cross leads us to a radical cultural change: the emergence of a mutuality culture in the midst of domination.

Jesus was a significant challenge to the culture of his day. His nonviolent approach allowed him to create more long-lasting change than if he were to have used violence. (How many violent revolutionaries have been so influential?) Nevertheless, after only a brief public career, he was killed by the Romans and their collaborators for being the subversive that he was. They saw him as a revolutionary, but they may not have realized how deep his revolution went. He was not seeking to change who was on top, but to create a humanity in which no "top" existed. He wanted to change the game in a fundamental way.

Jesus used images such as salt, leaven, light, and mustard seed to describe the way in which his apprentices would lead. They would transform the loaf like leaven, enliven the food like salt, bring renewed vision and sight to others, and function like a noxious weed in the fields now owned by the Romans. His strategy was to transform domination from within, not to take it by force.

He sent his apprentices into the world to proclaim and inaugurate the Reign of God, as he did. He called his apprentices to practice baptismal awareness and to engage in risky behavior on behalf of God's Reign of Mutuality.

> Jesus said to them again, 'Peace be with you. As the Father has sent me, so I send you.' (John 20:21)

In recent decades, liberation theologians have reminded us of the nonviolent public leadership of Jesus. Others have maintained that Jesus is primarily a spiritual teacher—that is, he teaches us what it means to be human as individuals. I see these two as inseparable. Without honoring the nonviolent public leadership of Jesus, we diminish God's concern for the living conditions of human beings, as God exhibited in the Exodus. Without honoring the spiritual depth of Jesus' life and teachings, we empty any real change of its center, essential methods, and direction.

Baptismal awareness can lead us to engage in nonviolent public leadership. Harvard Professors Ronald Heifetz and Martin Linsky propose that leadership is the act of providing orientation to a group of people.[23] Walter Brueggemann writes that the church's public message "is aimed simply and solely at summoning people to new, liberated obedience to the true governor of all created reality."[24] The leadership of Jesus, then, is to provide a new orientation to people, helping them move from the reign of domination to the God's Reign of Mutuality.

Many understand "leadership" as authoritarian—that is, an exercise of dominance over subservient others. Jesus' expression of leadership was something quite different: He oriented people to the inbreaking reign of God and inviting them to become full partners with him in that reign.

To faithfully follow Jesus means to engage in both dimensions of Jesus' invitation: baptismal awareness and nonviolent public leadership.

Without the spiritual depth of Jesus' proposal for how we can handle human existence, any true change is impossible. This spiritual depth is necessary if we are to avoid the historical pattern of human revolutions: The right becomes the wrong, the left becomes the right.[25]

God's Reign of Mutuality is both emerging and inbreaking. It is emerging from the creation of God and inbreaking from the One who created it. If it is not capable of emerging from creation, then it is not possible here. If it is not inbreaking, then it is susceptible to all the maladaptive ways of culture. Because it is both, we have reason to work and hope in the name of Jesus. God both facilitates and leads our participation in the healing of the world.

Courage

How did Jesus come to embrace his mortality and life, his strength and vulnerability? There is no doubt it takes courage to embrace our impossible situation. But once embraced, what then?

Just before his explanation of what it means to be his apprentice, Jesus outlined his own story as he understood it.

> The Son of Man must undergo great suffering, and be
> rejected by the elders, chief priests, and scribes, and be
> killed, and on the third day be raised. (Luke 9:22)

Jesus recognized, as did everyone else in his culture, that engagement in nonviolent public leadership within the Roman Empire would lead to one punishment: death. He experienced deep anxiety about this, as we see in several accounts of his prayer among the oil presses of Gethsemane.

In the midst of this anxiety, however, Jesus was affirmed by the God of Life and given courage to live, really live, despite knowing of his own immanent death. This affirmation is different from the affirmation of culture in two ways: 1) It comes in the moment when we consciously recognize our true condition, and 2) it is pure gift that comes from somewhere beyond us. Embracing our true condition and realizing that we are embraced by God is the key to a truly authentic life.

In the midst of his despair when confronting his own death and limitation, Jesus recognized a resounding "Yes" from the Creator of all. Obedience to this One is what makes for truly liberated life. Jesus' life as a vulnerable and mortal creature was affirmed, and his death would not be the last word from the God who creates and sustains life.

In J.K. Rowling's deeply Christian series, *Harry Potter*, Dumbledore speaks of the differences between Harry and his nemesis, Voldemort:

> "You are the true master of death, because the true master of death does not seek to run away from Death. He accepts that he must die, and understand that there are far, far worse things in the living world than dying."[26]

What makes Harry different from Voldemort is that Harry has the courage to face death. Voldemort's cowardice leads him to dominate and destroy all those around him. What Harry did in fiction, Jesus did in real life.

Jesus did not deny or try to avoid his death with the promise of resurrection. He saw in the promise of resurrection the same affirmation we find in the creation story's "good, very good," God's heart of compassion for the slaves in Egypt, and the prophets' call to justice and mercy for all God's people. He saw, as Dr. Martin Luther King, Jr. saw, that the long arc of the universe moves in the direction of justice for all people and that our truest purpose is to lend our fragile strength to God's arm.

Salvation

Having discussed sin as a gut-level rejection of life-as-it is, I turn to what "salvation" might mean. In our culture, salvation is a term that is nearly broken. It is frequently understood to mean going to heaven when you die because you agree with the theology of a particular church or have an experience approved by a church. It is often understood that salvation is our entrance into heaven because Jesus finally talked God into forgiving us.

Many people think Christianity is about dealing with feelings of guilt. In Jesus, God does indeed seek reconciliation with and between all things. This is a crucial part of Christianity, but not the core. In Jesus, God responds to the central issue: Is life worth living at all?

In other words, how can human beings be reconciled to the life we have been given so that we can take part in God's reconciliation with all things? How can we embrace our vulnerability so that we can see the loveliness of life that lies beyond the armor of our insulation?

The scriptural meaning of salvation is "healing" or "wholeness." When Jesus announced that salvation had come to the house of Zacchaeus (Luke 19), he did not mean that he handed the man a ticket to heaven. Zacchaeus was living an allegiance to a worldview that separated him from himself, God, and his neighbor. Zacchaeus' invitation to Jesus and his commitment to change his way of life signaled that he had fundamentally changed his allegiance from one reign to another, from domination to mutuality. This brought Zacchaeus a healing that moved him towards wholeness. Salvation takes place in the here and now.

Both sin and salvation occur in the context of life-as-it-is: life riddled with anxiety created by the fact that life includes both vulnerability/death and a strong desire for life. Sin is a gut-level rejection of life-as-it-is, expressed by striving for power that leads to, or conforms to, domination/submission systems.

Salvation is, in the midst of our anxiety, being accepted by the God beyond our idea of god, which empowers our ability to embrace life-as-it-is and, in turn, to participate in God's Reign of Mutuality. Just as sin described both the personal rejection of life-as-it-it-is and our corporate domination culture, so salvation describes both our personal embrace of life-as-it-it-is and a culture changed from domination to mutuality.

A word of clarification is needed before we proceed further. Some might mistake the term life-as-it-is as acquiescence to the status quo, either in our own lives or in the societies that we participate in. Accepting life-as-it-is is the not same thing as accepting life as we live it, but leads us to deeply question life as we live it. Baptismal awareness leads us to a life-long repentance: turning around from a life of slavery to domination culture to discovery of our freedom to be who God has made us to be.

Salvation, as Paul and Luther both attest, is something that comes from outside and beyond us. It is a free gift, a gift without strings. It is grace. We cannot be its source because we are a source that ends. We cannot affirm ourselves in our anxiety of life-facing-death because death ends us. To say that human beings are the source of their own salvation is like saying it is possible for a ship in stormy seas to attach its anchor to itself in order to successfully avoid crashing into the rocks.

If, however, the Eternal One affirms our life, this is a different matter. The anxious sea still rages. Life continues to include both vulnerability/death and the desire for life. But now these two are held together in God's affirmation of life-as-it-is.[27] What sin tears apart, we now begin to experience as whole. The very anxiety we sought to avoid is now embraced as a part of a blessed life.

I used to think that I had so much anxiety as a child because I experienced multiple traumatic events. My parents' grocery store burned, ultimately resulting in bankruptcy. My mother was diagnosed with MS after years of fainting spells and the like. While these were important as occasions when anxiety was introduced into my particular story, anxiety about life-as-it-is is inescapable and inevitable.

For years I thought that Christianity was a way to do away with my anxiety, to solve it. This, too, was a rejection of life. Now I see that Christianity brings a way to consciously integrate anxiety into my life as the indivisible part of life that it is—life that is good, very good in the eyes of God.

It is okay to feel scared, lonely, and small. It is okay to be human.

One of the dangers here is that we could reduce the free gift of acceptance we call grace to the feeling of being embraced. God's grace is for us whether we feel it or not. We are embraced whether we feel God's arms or not. It is precisely when we are the most lonely and afraid and on the cross of our life that the crucified one is with us. The Eternal One anchors and embraces our life, no matter how the wind and waves batter us with fear.

Salvation has often been segmented into two parts in Christian theology. One part has been justification (God's free gift of acceptance of our life); the other, sanctification (the reforming of life based on this acceptance). I now think it time to express these terms differently:

- The question of justification: Is life worth living at all?
- The question of sanctification: Now that life is worth living, how can we express our God-given freedom in God's Reign of Mutuality?

Theologians sequence these two for very good reasons. As suggested above, we need the eternal to accept us. This cannot be based on something that we do or do not do. This acceptance must be a gift, and a gift given each moment. Even so, this gift changes things. Sanctification is not known in the absence of anxiety or the human tendency to reject life-as-it-is, but in an paradoxical ability to consciously hold anxiety and death as parts of life because we are lovingly held by God as creatures having anxiety. Sanctification is based on justification as walls are based on a foundation. It leads us to re-envision life and what life is for.

The free gift of grace is continually reconnecting us to our life-as-it-is. As God's grace has its way with us, we may find ourselves more able to embrace the life we have been given, including the anxiety created by our vulnerability and desire for life. We find that we are neither greater nor less than our neighbor. We find that we are able to more deeply sense and participate in God's Reign of Mutuality. Like Zacchaeus, we may find that our lives are changed and we are being healed toward wholeness. Morpheus has found us. Surprisingly, Morpheus is the Creator of All, who seeks to restore us to ourselves.

CHAPTER FIVE

Deeper Than Domination

A commonly held expectation of first-century Palestinians was that a messiah would come, raise an army, and lead the people of Israel in a war against Rome. Jesus had a different view. The Christian Scriptures are full of examples of Jesus' particular understanding of the messiah's role. I will focus on three.

Dismantling Domination

And Mary said,

> 'My soul magnifies the Lord, and my spirit rejoices in God my Savior, for he has looked with favor on the lowliness of his servant. Surely, from now on all generations will call me blessed; for the Mighty One has done great things for me, and holy is his name. His mercy is for those who fear him from generation to generation. He has shown strength with his arm; he has scattered the proud in the thoughts of their hearts. He has brought down the powerful from their thrones, and lifted up the lowly; he has filled the hungry with good things, and sent the rich away empty. He has helped his servant Israel, in remembrance of his mercy, according to the promise he made to our ancestors, to Abraham and to his descendants for ever.' (Luke 1:46-56)

In the Gospel of Luke, Mary goes to see her cousin Elizabeth and prays this prayer of gratitude when they meet. When she prays that God's mercy is for those who fear him, she does not mean that God has mercy on us when we feel threatened by God. Rather, "fear" of God is more like being "awestruck" of God—sensing the diversity and immensity of creation, the vastness of space, and experiencing the mysterious trembling that this awareness causes in us. This is a conscious experience of our mortality. This is what is meant by fear of the Lord being the beginning of wisdom. Yet the God revealed in the Exodus is tender towards us and does not hold our vulnerability in contempt.

Mary's prayer is not only about her individual experience. God is faithful to the "lowly ones" who embrace the power and weakness of our impossible situation even while in the midst of a domination culture. God scatters the proud, brings down the powerful from their thrones, and lifts up the lowly. In a culture of domination such as the Roman Empire, Mary gives thanks for both God's previous acts toward mutuality and those that will be begun in Jesus. God will dismantle domination by reordering society.

The poetry bears witness to radical changes aimed not at simply replacing those at the top, nor killing them, but doing away with domination altogether. The proud in the thoughts of their hearts will be scattered: the illusions of power that helped them to deny their own condition will be taken from them. Wealth—and with it, power—is just one form of affirmation that serves to insulate us from our true condition. The rich will be sent away empty: For the first time, they will sense their own mortality and limitation. This is not intended to curse them or describe the eternal situation of the proud and rich. Rather, the scattering and hunger of those at the top of the pyramid is a condition necessary for their acceptance of their own humanity.

> Then Jesus looked around and said to his apprentices,
> "How hard it will be for those who have wealth to enter
> the kingdom of God." (Mark 10:23)

It is difficult for the rich to enter the Reign of God not because God won't have them. They have given up life to avoid death by receiving affirmation through being rich. Money is not just currency for things; it is the currency of affirmation by culture. Their wealth and power are the tranquilizers to which they have become addicted. To change this will be tough. They will have to go cold turkey. But when they look up from the tomb of their lost cultural affirmation, they will see the mercy of God on the faces of their newly recognized brothers and sisters.

Jesus in the Wild

In a second example of Jesus' nonviolent messianic role, the gospel writers tell us a story about his vision and preparation for his public ministry:

> And when Jesus had been baptized, just as he came up from the water, suddenly the heavens were opened to him and he saw the Spirit of God descending like a dove and alighting on him. And a voice from heaven said, 'This is my Son, the Beloved, with whom I am well pleased.' Then Jesus was led up by the Spirit into the wilderness to be tempted by the devil. He fasted for forty days and forty nights, and afterwards he was famished. The tempter came and said to him, 'If you are the Son of God, command these stones to become loaves of bread.' But he answered, 'It is written, "One does not live by bread alone, but by every word that comes from the mouth of God."' Then the devil took him to the holy city and placed him on the pinnacle of the temple, saying to him, 'If you are the Son of God, throw yourself down; for it is written, "He will command his angels concerning you", and "On their hands they will bear you up, so that you will not dash your foot against a stone."' Jesus said to him, 'Again it is written, "Do not put the Lord your God to the test."' Again, the devil took him to a very high mountain and showed him all the kingdoms of the world and their splendor; and he said to him, 'All these I will give you, if you will fall down and worship me.' Jesus said to him, 'Away with you, Satan! for it is written, "Worship the Lord your God and serve only him."' Then the devil left him, and suddenly angels came and waited on him. (Matthew 3:13-4:17)

Jesus receives his baptism by John the Baptist and is called God's beloved son. This title is a quote from, and an allusion to, several well-known passages in Hebrew scripture. Psalm 2 is a coronation psalm in which the king of Israel was named God's son. In Exodus, the entire Hebrew people were named God's son. This title serves to say that Jesus is both the messiah (priest/king who will bring liberation to the Jewish people and lead them to restore the world) and the one who embodies the Jewish people as God intends them to be. Jesus is God's agent and a leader of change among the Jewish people towards a culture of mutuality that God is bringing.

Jesus as the son is beloved and well pleasing to God. This sounds very sweet. It is, but it conveys much more than a kindly sentiment. This affirmation by God recalls Isaiah 42, which is often called a suffering servant song. Isaiah's community of prophets reflected on their experience in Babylon. Some of them came to believe that God would free them from Babylon through nonviolent means. Many biblical scholars say that Christians were the first to use the suffering servant of Isaiah in reference to the messiah. Jesus was to be the messiah, freeing and leading the people in the creation of a mutuality culture, and was to do it through nonviolent means.

In one sentence, Jesus' full humanity is summarized: He is powerful (that is, he is a messianic priest-king), and he is vulnerable and mortal (that is, he will suffer). In hearing the voice come from heaven, he is invited to embrace the fullness of his situation: Life, created by God, is good and death is a part of it. Jesus is called to baptismal awareness in his experience of baptism.

The Gospel of Matthew continues with Jesus being led to the wilderness by the Spirit. This recalls the people of Israel who were taken into the wilderness for 40 years to learn to recover from domination in Egypt. Here, Jesus fasts for 40 days. (Few things get us in touch with our mortality as much as starvation. Most of us have trouble missing a meal or even altering our diet—let alone fasting for nearly six weeks!) Central to preparing for his role as the nonviolent messiah, Jesus is put in touch with his vulnerability and mortality.

Enter the tempter—the spokesperson for domination culture who lives in our minds, among our family members and friends, in our workplaces and in the media—leading us to deny life-as-it-is. Armed with three temptations, the tempter first asks Jesus to use his status as messiah to shorten his fast and ensure his life. Recognizing that some things are more important than merely staying alive, Jesus responds to this temptation with the idea that the only ideal worth striving for is God's ideal of love for all people.

Next, the tempter invites Jesus to make a public display of his status as messiah. If many people saw him jump off the temple and be saved by angels, they would surely see him as the messiah. (On the downside, were this to happen, Jesus would be forced to live by their expectations of a violent messiah, thereby enshrining violence and domination as God's way.) As happened in the wilderness after Egypt (Exodus 17), this would be placing the expectations of people over God's vision for a new humanity. Another significant aspect of Jesus' response to this temptation is that by rejecting the stage show of a temple jump, he resists using the part of culture we call religion to control people. Jesus resists the Egyptian, Babylonian, and Roman tools of mass control. He will lead from beside us and from among those at the bottom of the pyramid.

In the third temptation, Jesus is taken to "a very high mountain" to see all the kingdoms of the world. Mountains are often scriptural symbols for domination cultures—think of pyramids here. Being taken to a very high mountain,—that is, to the center of Roman hierarchy—is a poetic way of saying that Jesus is taken to Rome, from where he can see all the embassies of occupied territories within the Roman Empire. If Jesus will worship the tempter, the ways of domination and denial, he will be able to replace those at the top of the domination culture. As we will see in the next chapter, God is not seeking to replace those at the top of domination. In the Exodus story, God sought to free his people from domination, not make them dominant over others.

Jesus' response to these temptations reveal much about his vision of leadership as an honest search for the deepest truth, embrace of our life-as-it-is, and striving for mutuality with others.

The gospel writers tell us that Jesus faced his mortality and vulnerability in the wilderness. He had the courage to face his own impossible situation, and that enabled him to resist both the ideals of Rome and those of his Jewish contemporaries who would either make war with Rome or submit to Rome in order to get along. Jesus was not interested in merely resisting Roman domination or giving credence to the imperial propaganda of the *Pax Romana*. His intention was to expose the Roman ideal of power as not worth living and to replace it with new beliefs, values, vision, and a new way of living.

Blessed Are the Vulnerable

Jesus gives his core teaching on how to be human in a world torn apart by denial and domination:

Then he looked up at his apprentices and said: 'Blessed
are you who are poor, for yours is the kingdom of God.
'Blessed are you who are hungry now, for you will be
filled. 'Blessed are you who weep now, for you will
laugh. 'Blessed are you when people hate you, and when
they exclude you, revile you, and defame you on account of the Son of Man. Rejoice on that day and leap
for joy, for surely your reward is great in heaven; for
that is what their ancestors did to the prophets. 'But
woe to you who are rich, for you have received your
consolation. 'Woe to you who are full now, for you will
be hungry. 'Woe to you who are laughing now, for you
will mourn and weep. 'Woe to you when all speak well
of you, for that is what their ancestors did to the false
prophets. (Luke 6:20-26)

Roman occupation included a system of economic exploitation and
domination that contributed to the death of many Palestinians. Most
of the wealth and cultural affirmation went to the top ten percent of
the population. Therefore, Luke's "poor" and Matthew's "poor in spirit"
refer to the same people: those who have died a cultural death. They have
neither been able to attain any ideal proposed by the domination culture
of the Romans nor attain the sub-cultural ideals proposed by the collaborating Jewish leadership. Jesus taught that while the poor were hungry,
their vulnerabilities exploited, and were held of no account in domination culture, a new day is coming. The cultural death that condemned
them has, in fact, prepared them for a new life. They have seen the lie of
power and now are able to see the world through different eyes. He called
them to hope—in real-world terms—that a new way of life was possible.

The term "son of man" is a powerful image from Ezekiel and Daniel. It
represents both God and those made in the image of God who are being
true to that image. Ezekiel looks up and sees a vision of God in the image
of a human. (When we see God's character, we see how we are called to
be.) Daniel picks up this theme in chapter seven. He writes that after all
the domination kingdoms of the world surround and persecute the son
of man (this time referring to the people of Israel), they would, one day,
stand up and be triumphant. He envisions the day when human beings
will be truly human and cast off the shroud of domination.

Jesus says that the poor and despised can begin to live that reality now.

They are now the "son of man" and are joining Jesus as the embodiment of the son of man. Having faced their vulnerability and mortality, they will be able to live differently. This passage also reveals that they can have something else: hope. They can believe that the character of God was revealed in the Exodus from Egypt and that God's true character—and therefore the true character of the universe, and therefore the true character of human beings—is not denial and domination. Domination cultures may reign for a while. On a given day, domination may win. But they will not win in any ultimate way or in any ultimate sense, for the God who created the universe is moving to reorder how we live. We now live by and the through hope for God's Reign of Mutuality.

We are so used to hearing the terms "son of god" and "son of man" that we do not think to give pause as to what these terms meant to Luke's first-century readers. They could rejoice because the son of man (God) was moving through the son of man (Jesus) to lead the son of man (his apprentices) to restore the world to mutuality. By calling apprentices, he was creating a messianic community that would continue and expand his work, and local bodies within the messianic community that would lead locally. They would be different, living out more closely God's vision for human beings. They would live by a different worldview and hold a different allegiance. But they would do all this in contact with the domination culture around them. This would lead them to claim their humanity and embody God's Reign of Mutuality in the midst of the Roman Empire. These local parts of Jesus' messianic community would be freed up to act as nonviolent change agents in their location.

How differently would they live?

> 'But I say to you that listen, Love your enemies, do good to those who hate you, bless those who curse you, pray for those who abuse you. If anyone strikes you on the cheek, offer the other also; and from anyone who takes away your coat do not withhold even your shirt. Give to everyone who begs from you; and if anyone takes away your goods, do not ask for them again. Do to others as you would have them do to you. 'If you love those who love you, what credit is that to you? For even sinners love those who love them. If you do good to those who do good to you, what credit is that to you? For even sinners do the same. If you lend to those from whom you

> hope to receive, what credit is that to you? Even sinners
> lend to sinners, to receive as much again. But love your
> enemies, do good, and lend, expecting nothing in re-
> turn. Your reward will be great, and you will be children
> of the Most High; for he is kind to the ungrateful and
> the wicked. Be merciful, just as your Father is merciful.
> (Luke 6:27-36)

Apprentices are to live so differently that instead of hating or killing their enemies, they will love them. Here, "love your enemies" does not necessarily mean to feel warm and fuzzy affection for them. It means to treat them well and seek their wellbeing. Jesus calls us to be merciful to those who have been captivated by denial and domination. To respond to them with violence is not simply morally wrong, it affirms the worldview of denial and domination. The way we respond to the violence of one deemed an enemy is to make a theological statement about the way the world is. Jesus called his apprentices to announce the reign of God's mutuality in their practical response to violence.

In the first-century Mediterranean world, a social superior would slap a slave with the back of his hand. Once this happened, to turn one's cheek invited a slap from the palm of the hand——something only done to equals. The act of turning one's cheek when struck was a way to claim one's dignity and invite the other to move from domination to mutuality. Hence, this was a active, nonviolent response to the dehumanizing teeter-totter of the Roman Empire.

Few things may demand our attention more than the presence of an enemy, but such illusions only serve to numb us to our real pain. While we might like to think that we suffer only because of our enemy, this is truly not the case. When we realize that our enemy shares the same condition we have, we realize that our combatant status is a tranquilizing distraction from our real problem. Jesus is calling his apprentices to practice compassion (to suffer with) for all people, including enemies.

Culture and the Challenges that Face Us

Human beings face challenges significant enough to call our very survival into question. These challenges cannot be met with the use of mere technology. If human beings respond to culture in the way I am proposing, we would deal with these challenges by learning how to handle the central dynamic of life: our impossible situation. If we do not, the maladaptive "solutions" of culture may, in fact, come home to roost. They have in many places and at many times before.

Here is one way to name the challenges:

- How do we understand and manage life and death as human beings?
- How do we live together despite significant differences of worldview and culture?
- How will we live on this planet in a way that respects the ecosystem and those who will live after us?

Jesus was trying to teach his apprentices a way to handle differently the central human dynamic of our simultaneous desire for life and anxiety over vulnerability and death. Because rejecting life-as-it-is would make us more susceptible to domination culture, he taught a baptismal awareness of practicing the embrace of both life and death.

Because he practiced baptismal awareness, he could resist the ways in which culture can be maladaptive. He could resist the full body cast that could have kept him from being who he was. He could cut the cultural strings that threatened to control him and see through the cultural blindness that said his was the best of all possible cultures. Because he embraced life and death every day, he had less unconscious energy built up in him, and so he could resist destructive discharge, with its scapegoating and violence against those perceived as different. Because he was learning to accept life-as-it-is, he did not allow himself feelings of guilt and shame whose function was to mask anxiety. Nor did he engage in the fantasy that he was powerless to participate with God in bringing a different kind of culture.

A Different Way to Be Human

Jesus was a radical human. He taught us to be human in a different way. He taught us to embrace our true human condition with baptismal awareness and to participate in God's Reign of Mutuality. He opened a window into God's vision for our lives and for our world.

Jesus teaches us an affirmation of our life that is based not on how well we live up to standards set by others but in the love given by the Creator of the cosmos, in whose eyes we are beautiful.

Jesus teaches a freedom from the ideals of denial and domination culture. He teaches a freedom for a life of enjoyment and loving service.

Jesus teaches expanded values that include all of life and all people and cultures, made possible when we are no longer protecting ourselves from our real condition by wanting to kill or convert those who are different.

Jesus teaches us that when we are not trying to distract ourselves from the life in which we find ourselves, we can better appreciate each moment; and when we are conscious of the fact that life is a gift that expires, every experience is savored.

Jesus teaches his apprentices a way to approach life in a way that frees us to respond to the environmental challenges of our time, no longer seeking the Jones's approval for the size of our house and how much stuff we can acquire/consume. In fact, Jesus teaches a freedom that might lead us to happily downsize and find that life is less complicated without all the frou-frou with which we have sought our internalized culture's approval. (All of this stuff requires its own pound of flesh, after all.)

Jesus teaches us that God is working among us to bring God's dream for humanity into reality. He shows us that we are invited to participate in realizing this dream without carrying the full burden of responsibility for the vision. He revealed how we are free to risk on behalf of this dream without either denying death or having a death wish.

Where did Jesus get this perspective?

It grew from the experience and spirituality of the people of Israel. Let's look at their story next

CHAPTER SIX

God Turns the World Upside Down

The ancient Egyptians lived in a world of order. This order was the ma'at (divine order) that encompassed all of earth and sky, human, animal, and plant. It was so much a part of the fabric of life that there was no separate word for "religion." This order symbolized and was maintained by the descendants of the gods we know as Pharaohs. When the Pharaoh dominated the population or other nations, the ma'at was affirmed. The world would be right when all people were brought into the order of the gods. The Pharaoh's job was to destroy chaos with the ma'at of the gods.

Within this "divine" order, all people knew their place. While they might not have been Pharaoh or one of his central counselors, they participated in this order and so found meaning in their lives. Even though each was mortal and would die, their culture would not; and if they fulfilled the role given them through this order, they would go on to the blessings of eternal life. They believed that they would say before the judgment throne of Osiris: "O far Strider, who came forth from Heliopolis, I have done no falsehood; Oh Fire-embracer who came forth from Kheraha, I have not robbed. I am not known to the director of servants."[28] Whether the Egyptians actually faced Osiris in judgment, the story undoubtedly had its effect—motivation to be an ideal slave.

This prayer taught them that the gods demanded their submission to the order set forth by the Pharaoh, and that this order was itself of divine origin and could not be questioned. Furthermore, the prayer's setting was before Osiris after their death. This was a not-so subtle reminder of mortality. As researchers have found, reminders of mortality have the powerful effect of making us cling more tightly to our culture.

When faced with other cultures and people, Egyptians had a typical human response: desire to conquer them in one way or another.

> Now a new king arose over Egypt, who did not know Joseph. He said to his people, 'Look, the Israelite people are more numerous and more powerful than we. Come, let us deal shrewdly with them, or they will increase and, in the event of war, join our enemies and fight against us and escape from the land.' Therefore they set taskmasters over them to oppress them with forced labor. They built supply cities, Pithom and Rameses, for Pharaoh. But the more they were oppressed, the more they multiplied and spread, so that the Egyptians came to dread the Israelites. The Egyptians became ruthless in imposing tasks on the Israelites, and made their lives bitter with hard service in mortar and brick and in every kind of field labor. They were ruthless in all the tasks that they imposed on them. (Exodus 1:8-14)

A threat to the divine ma'at was now growing like a tumor within the Egyptian culture: A people more numerous and potentially more powerful than they was now living among them. This threat would need to be dealt with if they hoped to preserve their cultural insulation. They sought to re-establish the divine order of things and safeguard the meaning of their lives by choosing a shrewd strategy: They would enslave the offspring of Joseph and his family. Numerous resident aliens were to be feared as a threat to the eternal order. However, numerous obedient slaves would be proof of their culture's power. Denial and domination culture is particularly susceptible to this kind of violent response to others—the violent response was slavery.

To reduce the risk of armed insurrection, Pharaoh ordered the midwives to kill all the newborn males of the Israelites. He ordered genocide. When the midwives resisted this, Pharaoh decreed that every Israelite male born was to be thrown into the Nile. The story says that the midwives "feared God"—that is, they held an ideal that was higher than Pharaoh. Moses was born and sent down the river, only to arrive in Pharaoh's household and be raised as a son.

Moses killed an Egyptian overseer and then escaped to Midian, where he found a wife and began the work of a shepherd.

> After a long time the king of Egypt died. The Israelites groaned under their slavery, and cried out. Out of the slavery their cry for help rose up to God. God heard their groaning, and God remembered his covenant with Abraham, Isaac, and Jacob. God looked upon the Israelites, and God took notice of them. (Exodus 2:24-25)

Moses' attention was attracted by a bush that burned but was not consumed. In the next verses, we see into the heart of God as understood by the Jewish people:

> Then the Lord said, 'I have observed the misery of my people who are in Egypt; I have heard their cry on account of their taskmasters. Indeed, I know their sufferings, and I have come down to deliver them from the Egyptians, and to bring them up out of that land to a good and broad land, a land flowing with milk and honey. (Exodus 3:7-8)

In the imagination of the Hebrew storyteller, the very center of God's character is to know the sufferings of the oppressed and to empower their freedom through a renewed vision. Note how different this is from the character of the ma'at of the ancient Egyptians.

The Carrot and the Stick

Domination cultures use both military and religious means to ensure the order. According to the ma'at, Pharaoh is a descendent and agent of the god Ra and so cannot be resisted any more than can the very forces of life and death. The Egyptian army and the slaves' taskmasters made sure to back up this power.

Of the two powers, military and religious, religious power was more effective in terms of both control and managing cost. Utilizing the religion of their divine order, the Egyptian leadership was able to control the population through their imagination of what it meant to human and humanity. They did this by using a religious cultural narrative that served to turn humans into marionettes. Today we have other means of forming the sense of the ideal (movies, television, books, sports), but back then, large gatherings that featured religious rituals were the primary means of forming the narrative of the ideal for any culture.

Again, the Prayer of the Dead reminded the Egyptians of their death and that certain things were expected of them in living up to the cultural ideal. Because death was brought closer to their conscious awareness, they were more likely to respond with a desire to protect their culture and do what they were asked to do.

A person born as a slave may not like it and may wish to have some other role in society. However, if she is a slave "because the gods made her this way," then she has no choice other than to be all she can be as a slave. The full body cast constricts her, but at least she gets insulation from her terror of being human and a sense of meaning as she participates in a culture that is much larger than she is and will certainly outlast her. The Egyptian leaders were able to enforce their domination on their own and other populations because human beings are willing to trade freedom for culturally blessed meaning to avoid dealing with the conflict of being human.

Participants in Egyptian society received insulation from the daily emotional awareness of their impossible situation in return for their own freedom. Their culture gave them a sense that their lives were of significance when they did their assigned tasks well. Their culture gave them an ideal and affirmation for fulfilling that ideal. Those who resisted this ideal and the affirmation it offered felt as though they had died.

Not at Any Cost

The Hebrew proposal is that God does not bless every order. Human culture with meaning for humans and order for communities is a good thing—but not at any cost.

The key insight of the Hebrew people into the nature of God (and therefore the true nature of the universe) is that God seeks to create an order of mutuality, not domination. To facilitate this, God was willing to lead this change by calling leaders like Moses to free people from slavery and begin to learn how to live differently. This way of life was spelled out in a covenant with God and written into the instruction, or Torah, of God.

The mutuality culture enshrined in this covenant would propose a very different meaning for human life and human community. Instead of constantly competing to have more than our neighbor, we live meaningfully when we are satisfied with what we have. (Exodus 20:17) Instead of looking for people to exploit, we are to care for the orphan, widow, and the immigrant. (Exodus 22:21-22) Instead of the rich getting richer, we are to arrange our economic life so that all are food secure. (Exodus 23:10-11, Leviticus 25) Instead of getting every last hour out of the people who work for us, we are to give them a day off for enjoyment, reflection, and rest. (Exodus 23:12) Instead of worshiping a God whose character is to dominate, we worship a God who rescues the slave.

At the heart of the Hebrew Bible is a God who proposes a mutuality culture in the midst of a culture of domination.

Cross-Cultural Document

The Hebrew Bible certainly contains many stories and teachings that do not seem to fit with the thesis of God proposing a mutuality culture. To deeply respect these scriptures and the people who wrote them, we would need to look at each one in its own historical and cultural context. We could then compare these stories and teachings to those of other cultures in the region. We find one example in the teaching in Exodus 21: "an eye for an eye and a tooth for a tooth." We clearly would reject this as a moral teaching today. In its time, however, it was a big step forward. At the time of this teaching's introduction, tribes were the only source of protection for their people. When a person of another tribe hurt one of their own, they were honor bound to give escalating retribution against members of the other tribe. The other tribe would then be honor bound to do the same, potentially leading to a full-scale conflict. In its day, this teaching served to limit this escalation. This is why, despite its unsuitability for our use, this teaching was a move toward mutuality in its own cultural context.

The writers and editors of the Hebrew Bible also knew that human beings were all too susceptible to domination. The writers attempted to be honest about this in their recollection and critique of the history of Israel. Much of the story of the Hebrew Bible centers on a mutuality culture being subverted to become a domination culture and then attempting to recover mutuality.

Seeing the Big Picture

Our culture has so poorly understood the key message of the "Old Testament" that it is necessary to reread and retell these stories in light of their meaning within their cultural context. To say that our culture disrespects the Hebrew Scripture is a vast understatement. When our larger culture tells you something about a Biblical text, study it for yourself.

In Samuel's day, the people asked him for a king who would rule over them so they could be like the other nations. Samuel prays to God, and this is what God says a king will do:

> He said, 'These will be the ways of the king who will reign over you: he will take your sons and appoint them to his chariots and to be his horsemen, and to run before his chariots; and he will appoint for himself commanders of thousands and commanders of fifties, and some to plough his ground and to reap his harvest, and to make his implements of war and the equipment of his chariots. He will take your daughters to be perfumers and cooks and bakers. He will take the best of your fields and vineyards and olive orchards and give them to his courtiers. He will take one-tenth of your grain and of your vineyards and give it to his officers and his courtiers. He will take your male and female slaves, and the best of your cattle and donkeys, and put them to his work. He will take one-tenth of your flocks, and you shall be his slaves. And in that day you will cry out because of your king, whom you have chosen for yourselves; but the Lord will not answer you in that day.' (1 Samuel 8:11-18)

Even so, as the text goes on to say, the people wanted a king and so they got one. The long, slow slide into domination/submission began anew.

The Hebrew Bible does not portray God as giving up, however strong the warning through Samuel. God continued to send truth tellers, or prophets, to restore the people to a culture of mutuality. Read, now from Isaiah, a common theme of the prophets:

> Ah, you who make iniquitous decrees, who write oppressive statutes, to turn aside the needy from justice and to rob the poor of my people of their right, that widows may be your spoil, and that you may make the orphans your prey! What will you do on the day of punishment, in the calamity that will come from far away? To whom

will you flee for help, and where will you leave your
wealth, so as not to crouch among the prisoners or fall
among the slain? For all this, his anger has not turned
away; his hand is stretched out still. (Isaiah 10:1-4)

Isaiah spoke these words of truth in order to provoke a change from a
culture that, while claiming faithfulness to God, used their laws and their
government to create a domination culture.

Worse, the people used the very worship of God as cover for the domination culture they had created. Again, they were using religion to shackle
the imagination of the population, but the truth tellers would out them:

I hate, I despise your festivals, and I take no delight in
your solemn assemblies. Even though you offer me your
burnt-offerings and grain-offerings, I will not accept
them; and the offerings of well-being of your fatted animals I will not look upon. Take away from me the noise
of your songs; I will not listen to the melody of your
harps. But let justice roll down like waters, and righteousness like an ever-flowing stream. Amos (5:21-28)

The covenant of mutuality with God had been distorted to become
another version of ma'at. Again and again, the prophets came and spoke
a harsh word of truth so that the Hebrew people might change.

'With what shall I come before the Lord, and bow myself before God on high? Shall I come before him with
burnt-offerings, with calves a year old? Will the Lord be
pleased with thousands of rams, with tens of thousands
of rivers of oil? Shall I give my firstborn for my trans-
gression, the fruit of my body for the sin of my soul?'
He has told you, O mortal, what is good; and what does
the Lord require of you but to do justice, and to love
kindness, and to walk humbly with your God? (Micah
6:6-8)

A faithful remnant always existed among the people of Israel, despite
the power of domination culture to assimilate or dismiss those who held
God's vision of mutuality and dismiss or subvert that vision. Their faith
in the God of mutuality was tested by both internal and external threats.
When the Babylonians took them into exile in Babylon, beginning in 603
BCE, they again faced slavery in a domination culture. The Babylonians

believed that human beings were made for the express purpose of being slaves. Their creation story said that the world was the rotting body of the gods' mother, Tiamat, who had been killed by one of the gods in battle. The gods made humans from the dead body of Tiamat to be slaves and work the irrigation fields. The king, being an agent of the gods, was to keep order and conquer those nations that did not adhere to this reality.

Remembering as an Act of Resistance

Enslaved in Babylon, the Jewish people engaged in an act of remembrance and imagination of God's vision for the world. Though held captive, they refused to submit to the domination culture of the Babylonians and claimed an alternate story of the way things really are:

- The first story of creation. The God they knew created people to be God's agents in caring for one another and the creation as a whole. It is worth reading Genesis 1 through 2:4a to see how different their vision of the world and human beings was from the Babylonian creation story.
- The story of Exodus and the God who had freed them once before and who would free them once again.
- Their own self-critique as to why they were so vulnerable to the Babylonians (Isaiah, Jeremiah, Ezekiel).

During the Babylonian Exile, most of the Hebrew Scripture was written down so that this vision might not be lost. The vision held that God's promises to Abraham—his descendants would be a blessing to all nations (Genesis 12:1-4)—would be fulfilled. They dreamed that the people of Israel would live in such a way that others would want to emulate their non-domination way of life.

> In days to come the mountain of the Lord's house shall be established as the highest of the mountains, and shall be raised above the hills; all the nations shall stream to it. Many peoples shall come and say, 'Come, let us go up to the mountain of the Lord, to the house of the God of Jacob; that he may teach us his ways and that we

may walk in his paths.' For out of Zion shall go forth instruction, and the word of the Lord from Jerusalem. He
shall judge between the nations, and shall arbitrate for
many peoples; they shall beat their swords into plow-
shares, and their spears into pruning hooks; nation shall
not lift up sword against nation, neither shall they learn
war any more. (Isaiah 2:2-4)

Isaiah envisioned a day when all nations would stop worshiping domination, resulting in the end of war. The world would be restored to God's
intention in its creation. Soon, they reminded one another, the exile
would be over. God would lead them by straight paths, and they could
work to rebuild a culture of mutuality. After generations of waiting, the
Hebrew people did go home, in 640 BCE. They hoped that Isaiah's vision
would come true.

However, within a few centuries they were again conquered. In 63
BCE, the Romans took over. This time the Exile had come home.[29]

Denial and domination culture, with its proposal that to be truly human is to be powerful, has been around for at least 5,000 years. Many
such cultures have come, done their damage, and died. They have used
both religion and military to keep their populations under control. The
military makes them feel safe from outward enemies and subdues internal ones. The religion affirms the culture as ideal and lifts up what is ideal
for the human beings within the culture. Again, it would be easy for us to
imagine that these cultures arrive like an invading race from outer space.
Not so. Denial and domination cultures emerge from and are energized
by our rejection of life-as-it-is, which is the heart of the Christian word
"sin." Culture then lives out this sin on an immense scale that reinforces
it. Only a proposal that teaches us a different way to be human and frees
us up to confront large-scale cultural systems will help us be more truly
human.

Jesus began, or continued, from the heart of the Hebrew Scriptures
and their witness to the God of mutuality who works as a catalyst to
bring change the world. Jesus sought to lead us to be human and humanity in a way that more truly reflects the One in whose image we are made.
This way involved developing a deep, spiritual response to our situation
and partnering in allegiance to the Reign of Mutuality, which would
transform the ways of the world. He would be resisted on both proposals.

CHAPTER SEVEN

Living in the Reign of God

The Roman Empire was named after Romulus, who, according to legend, was one of the twin boys fathered by Mars, the god of war. The king of the region had decreed that the twin boys and their mother were to be killed through exposure in the river Tiber, but the gods kept them safe and provided a she-wolf to nurse them until they were found by a local shepherd. After the tyrant who had ordered their execution died, they were asked to be kings over the city. However, they soon entered into a bitter disagreement over where a new city should be founded, and Romulus killed Remus. Thus, the city was named Rome. According to legend, Romulus did not die, but was taken to heaven in a cloud—a sign that he was the ideal powerful human and Rome the ideal powerful society. The story a culture uses to describe its origins says a lot about its vision of the ideal human.

Rome became an empire during the rule of Augustus Caesar. Despite his flowery titles—savior of the world, prince of peace, and son of god—Augustus Caesar was just another figurehead of domination. He used many of the same tools the Egyptians and Babylonians had used—military, religion, and economic power—to conquer, control colonies, and extract as much wealth as possible. This was the empire's right, he thought, and the essence of what it means to be human. He later took the title "son of god" to make the claim that the empire's way was the way of the universe as ordained by the gods.

It was Caesar's policy to respect the local customs of Roman occupied lands. However, in a time when the worship of multiple gods was the norm, he expected to be worshiped as well. Caesar gave the Jews special permission not to worship him due to the Jewish unwillingness to worship multiple gods. This sounds rather nice. It must be noted, however, that the Romans chose the Jewish high priest and held his vestments under lock and key. Furthermore, whenever the high priest did not keep his fellow Jews under control to Rome's satisfaction, Caesar would choose a new high priest. In any event, what was once a right was now granted as a favor.

Israelites on their way to Jerusalem for the Passover would see other Jews hung, often naked, on Roman crosses, which, in first-century Palestine, would bring shame on all who saw them. The crucified would often be left to decay on the crosses and would not be buried. All this was Rome's way to remind the Jews that, while Yahweh was their God, it was Caesar's will that ruled.

Exile at Home

One of my favorite biblical scholars, N. T. Wright, names this period in Jewish history the "Exile at Home." It was felt in every part of life in Palestine. For the 90 percent of the people then living on a subsistence income, Roman taxes and the newly added temple tax took up nearly 38 percent of their income[30]—with few services offered in return, unless you count as a service the presence of an occupying and oppressive army and roads created not to build the infrastructure for the economy, but to ensure the army could move at a reliable pace in any kind of weather.

Roman control over the fishing industry of the Sea of Galilee exemplifies how the Romans used economics to control its conquered people and extract their wealth. We imagine that Peter, James, and John were fishing entrepreneurs, catching fish and then returning to the village to sell their catch on the open market. This was far from the case. By law, Caesar owned the water and all that was in it. One was punished severely for catching a fish without the proper license. The regional governor was given franchise over the fishing industry. He had ranks of people working beneath him who taxed the fish at every transaction. The regional governor charged fishing syndicates money to fish. In turn, each syndicate charged each family who wanted to fish. Each catch was taxed when it was caught, again when it was cleaned, again when it was transported, and again when it was sold.[31] When the gospel writers portray Jesus as catching and serving fish beside the sea, they reveal that he engaged in acts of civil disobedience—in this case, catching and serving untaxed and therefore stolen fish.

The domination culture of the Roman Empire brought ever increasing desperation to all the residents of Palestine. During the century before Jesus' arrest, land was gradually taken from common people through tax liens and given to those with Roman allegiance. By Jesus' day, only three people owned all the land in Galilee.[32] Many men were forced to go to the marketplace each day and hope they would be hired. If they were, they were paid enough to live on for that day. If not, they went home hungry to their equally hungry families. Centuries earlier, Pharaoh had oppressed the Israelites by demanding production of more bricks and withholding the straw needed to do the job—this, he thought, would silence any troublemakers. In Jesus' time, the day laborers were placed in a similar situation.

Perhaps worse, the Jewish people oppressed one another—which is typical behavior of those who are themselves oppressed. Oppressors rely on the behavior of infighting to justify further oppression. Jesus did not critique his own people for following Torah—Jesus was a faithful Jew and followed the Torah. He did, however, criticize the subversion of its purpose to either promote domination or numb people to its existence.

The religious leaders used the ritual life of the people of Israel as a means to extract even more wealth from most of them. The temple tax, money changed at high exchange rates, and high prices for sacrificial animals are examples. Equally as oppressive was the religious leaders' insistence that Roman occupation was God's punishment to the people of Israel for their unfaithfulness. Six hundred thirteen laws had been identified within the Torah. Sinners were those who could not obey them all. Yet only members of the middle and upper classes could afford to pay the temple tax, make all the sacrifices, and obey all the purity laws. The Pharisees' movement functioned to blame and guilt the poor and destitute, who constituted 85 to 90 percent of the population during the Exile at Home. This is why Jesus said they "strained at gnats and swallowed camels."

In his leadership, Jesus was committed to addressing this oppression and exploitation. As a result, he was viewed as a threat to the Roman order and the Jewish religious leadership, which led to his execution.

Responses to the Exile at Home

Over time, Roman occupation led to some in the Jewish nation keeping their outward forms of worship and culture while inwardly accepting the Roman ideal of power. Some lived like the Romans through collaboration; others, through emulation; still others, through abject despair. Many held fast in their hope of making a faithful response to God and bringing the people of Israel to the inheritance of God's call for them to be a blessing.

The Collaborators: The high priest (chosen by Caesar), the chief priests (chosen by the Roman governor), the Sadducees, and the scribes comprise this group. Official leaders of the Jewish people, they were motivated by personal gain (and survival) as well as the Roman threat to temple worship. Willing to squash dissent and revolution in order to preserve their positions, they were first-class collaborators. Many Jewish men served in the military; estimates tell us that up to ten percent of the Roman army consisted of Jews. Jewish people also served in administrative functions for the empire.

The Purists: These are the Pharisees, who felt that if every Jew were devout by obeying all the dietary and ritual laws, God would act to end the exile at home. Obedience to these laws, however, was simply out of economic reach for most of the population because of the effects of Roman occupation. Hence, the Pharisees blamed those most victimized for being victimized. In this way they emulated, or at least echoed, the Roman way of domination.

The Violent Revolutionaries: Zealots were either planning and biding their time or conducting armed revolt against the Romans. They felt that if they started a revolt, surely God would join in their just cause and would act out God's wrath against the Romans. They wanted (like some Christians who hope for war in the Middle East so that Jesus will come again) to force God's hand into joining them in Holy War. In 67 CE, they began a revolution and won a brief time of freedom. This freedom ended in 70 CE, when the Romans killed many in Jerusalem (up to 1.1 million, according to Romano-Jewish historian Josephus) and destroyed the temple. The Zealots emulated the Romans in methodology and the worship of power.

The Essenes: These folk did not like any of the above responses. They felt that they needed to disconnect from the empire entirely and live in the desert, where they would foster a pure and separate community. Jesus may have been philosophically closest to the Essenes, but he did not share their lack of engagement with the Roman Empire—which, in the end, amounted to a form of passive collaboration.

Someday

To some degree, all of these responses indicate that the Jewish people felt they needed to wait until after the Roman domination culture was removed before God's mutuality culture could be lived out. Through its threat to temple worship, military intimidation, and economic deprivation, Rome controlled people through their imaginations. As such, it was difficult for them to imagine any transition from domination culture to the mutuality culture envisioned by God and hoped for by their ancestors.

Living within the Roman ideal of denial and domination, the Jewish people increasingly lived on the teeter-totter of dominance and submission. They ordered their own society into hierarchies—economically, socially, and religiously. The "sinners" the Pharisees were so hard on were simply those who did not have the wealth to pay the temple tax and obey all 613 laws considered necessary for purity and morality.

As in all denial and domination societies, most of the wealth and power was concentrated at the top: Those in the top 10 percent consumed two-thirds of the produce. (Compare this with 2007 U.S. economic statistics: the top 10 percent receiving fully half of all the income earned in the entire country, as much as the bottom 90 percent combined.)

What the Jewish people had envisioned happening at the end of the Babylonian captivity did not materialize; their captivity just took a different form. Yet most of them longed to live a different way and remembered the promises of God expressed through Isaiah and the other prophets. They kept hope alive and called their vision the "reign of God": the fulfillment of God's vision of a mutuality culture in which all share food, land, shelter, and dignity.

Hoped-For Messiah

During the two centuries before Jesus' birth, many Jews came to believe that God would send an "anointed one" to lead this transition. We call this person "the messiah" based on the Hebrew word for "anointed." "Christ" is the Greek word for anointed. In Hebrew tradition, as part of their coronations, kings were anointed with oil. High priests were sometimes anointed as well. The anointed one would be both king and high priest, and would lead the Hebrew people while fulfilling God's promise to be a blessing to all peoples.

The messiah was generally expected to be a military general. He would free the people of Israel through a violent overthrow, gathering an army to kill and cast out the Romans and end the Exile at Home. He would be such a good warrior that he would make the mountains red with the blood of the enemies! [33]

The bloodshed would be only in preparation for implementing the reign of God, into which the messiah would invite all people to participate in a new way of being human.

> It is too light a thing that you should be my servant to raise up the tribes of Jacob and to restore the survivors of Israel; I will give you as a light to the nations, that my salvation may reach to the end of the earth. (Isaiah 49:6-7)

A Typical First Century Jewish View of Transition from Domination to Reign of God

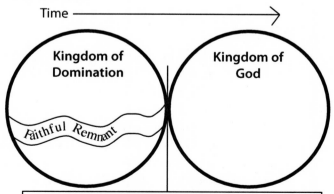

Time ⟶

Kingdom of Domination

Kingdom of God

Faithful Remnant

Messiah's Arrival:
Brings healing to Israel, raises an army and casts out empire, resurrects the faithful remnant, then brings healing to world

All the nations would learn how to live in a new way through the people of Israel. The messiah would heal the sick, release the political and religious prisoners, bring sight to the blind, and cleanse the lepers. (Isaiah 42:5-7) He would gather all the faithful to a wonderful feast (Isaiah 25), to which all nations would be invited.

In their emerging belief in salvation brought by an anointed one, first century Jews were plagued by a serious question of justice: What about the faithful who had died without seeing the rewards of the reign of God? Their response was that the messiah would resurrect the faithful remnant so that it could enjoy the mutuality culture in full flower.

They believed that in order to make all this happen, the messiah would have to use violence to overthrow the violence of the domination culture of the Roman Empire. The transition from reign of domination to reign of God would happen both violently and suddenly, with only a short time between the two reigns.

Jesus' Response

As Marcus Borg and N.T. Wright have written, Jesus was a revolutionary, revolutionary. He sought to bear witness to God's ways of transforming the world. He lead through evoking his people's various expectations for the messiah. He healed the sick, raised the dead, made the lame to walk, and held feasts to which all were invited. Through these various acts, Jesus claimed to be the messiah: He would lead his people to live as God had envisioned.

Toward achieving his goals, however, Jesus would use a methodology very different from what was expected.

Instead of killing his enemy, he loved his enemy and prayed for those who persecuted him. He healed the centurion's child and declared the centurion's faith to be great. He talked to Samaritans when good Jews were expected not to so much as even walk through Samaria. He talked to, debated with, and taught women—who were not supposed to engage in theology. He welcomed children, who (unlike children in our time) were not reckoned to be of any worth. He touched lepers (considered a serious affront to the purity laws, a sin) before he healed them. He even announced forgiveness of sins, often before any confession was made, and offered reconciliation with God without requiring the crushingly expensive sacrifices that were to be made in the temple. He engaged in nonviolent public leadership.

Jesus sought to redefine the messiah's job description, particularly insofar as the methods the messiah would use and who was to be included in the Reign of God. The gospels portray Jesus as a nonviolent public leader who inspired others to join him in his messianic work. He often asked people to keep quiet about the healing he had offered. Why? In New Testament scholarship, this question is called the "messianic secret." The people of Israel commonly expected a messiah to heal the sick, raise the dead, make the lepers walk, the blind to see, preach good news to the poor, and bring freedom to them by leading an army. Jesus was concerned that should word of his messiahship travel ahead of him too far, the common understanding of what was expected of the messiah would lead people to form an army. Jesus had to thread the needle, so to speak, to evoke their messianic expectations without showing up in Jerusalem only to find that they massed an army in his name. This army would then look to him as a general. If he refused, the army would find another messiah (which happened in 67 CE and 137 CE with disastrous consequences). Jesus wanted to make his proposal for another way to be human and humanity, and offer a different understanding of the messiah's role.

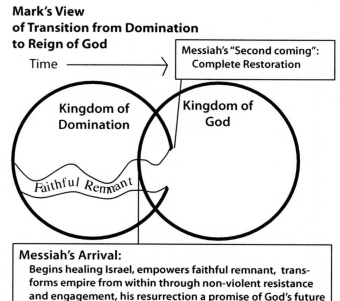

Mark's View of Transition from Domination to Reign of God

Time

Messiah's "Second coming": Complete Restoration

Kingdom of Domination

Kingdom of God

Faithful Remnant

Messiah's Arrival:
Begins healing Israel, empowers faithful remnant, transforms empire from within through non-violent resistance and engagement, his resurrection a promise of God's future healing for all

(I do not use the term messiah often in this book; instead, I use public leader, nonviolent leader, and so on. I choose these rather cumbersome words because our idea of the messiah's role is now as broken as the words "disciple" and "salvation": We commonly think that the messiah was the one who died talking God into forgiving us.)

Jesus' vision, according to the synoptic gospels, held that the new order of the reign of God was breaking into and simultaneously emerging from within, transforming the Roman Empire as leaven transforms bread and as seed transforms a landscape. Everyone was invited to participate. Lepers were touched, women became leaders, centurion's families were healed, and Samaritan women held their own in theological debate.

Jesus believed that the reign of God was near (Mark 1:14-14) and among (Luke 17:20-21) his followers. He formed his followers into a new culture of mutuality in the midst of the Roman culture of domination. People were not called to wait powerlessly and passively for God's reign, but to begin living it out in the midst of the Roman Empire and within a Jewish nation distorted and compromised by domination. By courageously embracing of human life-as-it-it-is, they would win over their enemy, because we are all family in the vision of God.

Our Exile at Home

Let's step back and look at this for a moment.

Jesus saw the devastation wrought by domination. He saw the increasing poverty, violence, and death caused by Roman domination culture, and he courageously sought to change the situation. He saw the interplay between individual human sin as rejecting life-as-it-is and our corporate sin of domination. Jesus' vision for apprentices was that they would continue his work through the practice of baptismal awareness and nonviolent public leadership in God's Reign of Mutuality until God's restoration of the world was complete.

He fundamentally rejected:

- collaboration with domination as a way to survive or have marginal influence
- purity movements that reduce God's Reign of Mutuality to belief in certain logical statements or the fulfilling of a list of requirements
- separatist movements that seek to create God's Reign

of Mutuality without engaging domination culture
- revolutionary movements that seek to use violence,
which only replaces who it is that dominates
- denial about or passive resignation to the status quo

He rejected them because all of these strategies leave domination culture intact. He envisioned small groups of people working like leaven in the dough to change domination culture from within.

While his movement has leavened the larger domination culture, it has so far failed to complete the transformation. For that we must await Jesus' "second coming," the time when he will complete this healing.

While the human race has made strides in human rights, participatory government, the rule of law and legal processes, and for negotiating our way through conflict, we continue to live in domination much more than we do in mutuality. Much of the time, we who claim Jesus as Lord have more in common with collaborators, purists, separatists, and violent revolutionaries than we do with Jesus. Many of us who quote the Bible, go to church, and preach in the pulpits of our congregations appear blind to his vision. We are blind because of the human tendency to reject our life-as-it-is and thus our susceptibility to cultures that promise power.

The purpose of a tradition is to keep a set of beliefs, values, and vision alive within a larger culture. A faith tradition, at its best, is intended to help the next generation see the power of sin and respond with some freedom to it and its effects. Yet within the first century of Christianity, Jesus' movement had lost its understanding of the specific problems that Jesus was addressing. Most of us want to be faithful to Jesus, we just don't have a good clue as to where Jesus is leading.

By the end of the first century, the Christian movement had lost much of the cultural memory needed to understand the writings whose authors sought to keep Jesus' vision alive. In the last 100 years, however, biblical scholars, anthropologists, sociologists, archeologists, historians, and linguists have helped us recover some of this cultural memory. We now know more about first-century culture than at any time since the close of that century. This does not mean that we can know for sure what Jesus was up to. Certainly his actions, words, and the accounts of his life we call gospels were all open to multiple meanings in their own time. However, because of this scholarly work, it is now possible to get a greater sense of what interpretations are plausible or not.

Many of those who went to Sunday school as children sang "Jesus Loves Me" and believed it. However, the problem that Jesus came to "fix" as proposed by our Sunday School teachers does not take into account all that Jesus faced in his first-century context. The problem, they taught, was that God could not forgive human beings. We were just too bad—but Jesus made it possible for God to forgive us. His death on the cross was necessary because God needed someone to pay for our sins. "God can't just forgive, God needs a perfect sacrifice to make up for all our sins," they would often say with a smile. And indeed, in accord with this line of thought, it was nice for God to have supplied the necessary perfect sacrifice. Nice and confusing!

Their interpretation is extraordinarily common. One can turn on a TV or radio and hear it every hour of the day. One can go to the supermarket and hear people repeat this interpretation. However, it does not seem to respect the breadth and depth of what we now understand about the message of the Christian Scriptures.

First, the notion of sacrifice taught in many Sunday schools, the media, and as understood on the street is simply not biblical. Sacrifice originated as a meal of reconciliation between tribes that were feuding. Each family would invite the other over for a good meal so that they could once again honor one another. Ancient peoples found this so powerful that they held meals of reconciliation with God. These people ate the meal, burning part of it to "send it up to God." This was an imaginative way to ritualize such reconciliation in a tribal, nomadic, herding culture.

The Hebrew theologians were clear that this meal did not change God, but rather it changed the people who shared it with God. Sacrifice is not a way to manipulate God. In Jesus' day, though, the leaders of the temple used the tradition of sacrifice as a means of exercising power over a tired, depressed, and hopelessly occupied nation. They provided a company store for forgiveness: They made forgiveness a commodity available only through them. When Jesus forgave people, often before they confessed any sin, he was boycotting the temple priests' purported ownership of reconciliation with God and neighbor.

Second, the notion of sin here is simply not biblical. God had a dream for a people who would be a blessing to all the peoples of the world (Genesis 12:1-4a). These people would live differently—they would be a shalom people. They would accept and celebrate their life as vulnerable and capable people. They would create a society of mutuality in which all would have enough. They would not lend money at interest, would keep part of their crop for the poor, and would return foreclosed land to its family in the year of Jubilee (Leviticus 25). They would treat their resident aliens with care, have a day for rest and enjoyment, and give the land rest every seventh year to respect the beauty of creation.

When John the Baptist and Jesus called for repentance of sin, they were not saying that the people should confess their mortality guilt. They were calling people to repent of their dominance and submission within the Roman denial and domination society. These leaders called the people of Israel out to the River Jordan. The Jordan was symbolically understood as the birth-place of their time in the land. To be baptized there signified that as a people they were making a new beginning. John and Jesus called them to repent of their sin: both their individual sin of rejecting life-as-it-is and the domination that results from it. They called the people of Israel back to their identity as shalom people and to once again live out mutuality in the midst of domination. By repenting of the teeter-totter of dominance and submission, they could once again carry the message of the good news of God's shalom to others.

The view espoused in Sunday schools and commonly understood in the larger media far too easily accommodates people to the denial and domination society in which we live. It leads people to remain in mortality guilt and shame instead hearing God's "Yes" in the midst of anxiety. It leads people to think that God needs violence, God needed to kill Jesus, in order to forgive. It misunderstands the wise teaching of our Hebrew theologians about the meaning of sacrifice. It minimizes (yes, minimizes) sin and repentance of sin into just feeling bad, when Jesus called us to a total change of worldview, allegiance, and way of living. Their teaching turns forgiveness in Jesus into the property of yet another company store. If Jesus resisted the use of forgiveness as the exclusive property of the temple priests, he would certainly resist churches who do the same.

The "problem" that Jesus addressed was specific to both the denial and domination plaguing the people in Palestine and remains universal in its application to the impossible situation of human beings. Jesus was trying to teach God's way of being human and being humanity, but he lived, as we all do, in a specific historical and cultural context.

Much of the Hebrew Scripture is the reflection by the people of Israel on how denial and domination cultures subverted God's vision of mutuality. In their writings and remembrances they sought to recover God's vision for human beings and human culture. Mutuality and acceptance were in constant flux with denial and domination. Christian history has been no different, except that, perhaps, we have not always confessed this as honestly as our Jewish sisters and brothers. All too often Christians are in our own exile at home: We reject the good gift of life in hopes that Jesus will beam us up soon. Christian language is used to blame and tame people into submission to authoritarian leaders. Christianity is used to bless or ignore the status quo of the moment, even when Jesus would clearly act and speak out against it.

Jesus calls us to allegiance to God and God's Reign of Mutuality. He calls apprentices to join him in baptismal awareness and to be salt, leaven, and seed, bringing nonviolent change to domination culture.

Jesus' Last Week

Living out a mutuality culture in the midst of Roman domination would mean engaging in a lot of conflict.

Jesus was in conflict with the Roman culture of domination. Much of this conflict is implicit in the images Jesus and the gospel writers used, and we have to work hard in order to understand enough about first-century culture to catch a glimpse of the radical challenge that Jesus represented. In their book, *The Last Week*, John Dominic Crossan and Marcus Borg explain what was at stake during Jesus' last week, into which he entered riding into town on a donkey.[34] Borg and Crossan help us to see that Jesus didn't do this because he liked parades.

Pontius Pilate lived in Caesarea by the Sea, where he could enjoy ocean breezes. During each of the main Jewish religious festivals, he marched garrison reinforcements into Jerusalem. He rode in on a fine horse, the very symbol of a conquering king in an imperial parade. Jesus rode into Jerusalem on a donkey, staging a counter-parade in protest of the Roman occupation of Palestine.

The crowds shouted "Hosanna to the son of David" as Jesus passed by. This was no accident. These words echo Psalm 118, used during the Passover meal, the *seder*. It was a way of saying that, because God was so certain that God would once again free them from slavery, they could already say "Thanks!" The check was not just "in the mail," it was in the mailbox. In their shouts, the crowds were participating in Jesus' counter-parade and protest, asserting their belief that, in Jesus, the mutuality culture of God's reign had begun and that Pilate's march into Jerusalem held no significance, other than to be mocked.

Even after this, Jesus did not retire for the day. He went directly to the temple and overturned the tables of the money changers and the animal vendors. Because most economic transactions required using Roman money and Roman currency was not allowed in the temple, the collaborating chief priests had set up a system whereby they could profit from currency exchange. They also profited from the high prices set for animals to sacrifice at the altar, claiming that the only way to be forgiven was via purchase of sacrificial animals purchased at the company store of the temple. Jesus challenged this domination-style move by offering forgiveness to people freely. In this protest, Jesus publicly challenged the Jewish religious leaders and exposed them in their roles as collaborators and unfaithful shepherds.

A Beginning

Jesus resisted domination culture in all its forms. His challenge to his culture was especially pronounced in that he engaged the conflict through nonviolent means. Of course, every conflict meant that Jesus threatened the Jewish leaders' cultural insulation. Jesus increased the tensions in an already tense situation. Imagine, celebrating freedom from slavery during the Passover while being an occupied people! Imagine how the political leaders felt, knowing they could not stop the celebration and fearful that people would find reason to hope for a different future.

The gospel writers are careful to say that Jesus' courageous public leadership would be the first in a movement, not a flash in the pan.

> In the morning, when he returned to the city, he was hungry. And seeing a fig tree by the side of the road, he went to it and found nothing at all on it but leaves. Then he said to it, 'May no fruit ever come from you again!' And the fig tree withered at once. When the disciples saw it, they were amazed, saying, 'How did the fig tree wither at once?' Jesus answered them, 'Truly I tell you, if you have faith and do not doubt, not only will you do what has been done to the fig tree, but even if

> you say to this mountain, "Be lifted up and thrown into
> the sea", it will be done. Whatever you ask for in prayer
> with faith, you will receive.' (Matthew 21:18-22)

Here, the fig tree symbolizes the whole of the people of Israel and God's hope that, by planting them in Palestine, they would bear fruit for all nations—that is, they would teach others to live in a mutuality culture. But Jesus, finding no fruit in the vineyard of the people of Israel—at least in the centers of power in Jerusalem—tells his apprentices that if they pray and believe, they can move mountains into the sea.

This does not mean what prosperity gospel preachers think it means. In the Bible, a mountain often symbolizes the political and cultural power of domination, as we saw in Jesus' temptations in the wilderness. Here, Jesus is encouraging his apprentices to trust enough to engage in the types of conflict required to bring about meaningful change.

Jesus' apprentices were to live in healing conflict with their Jewish sisters and brothers. They were to engage publicly in nonviolent resistance to domination. This would hurt feelings, challenge attitudes, and alter expectations, but the enemy was not the people. The culprit was the culture of domination that held and possessed them all.

> For our struggle is not against enemies of blood and
> flesh, but against the rulers, against the authorities,
> against the cosmic powers of this present darkness,
> against the spiritual forces of evil in the heavenly places.
> (Ephesians 6:12)

In his series on *The Powers*, Walter Wink wrote that domination systems warp and ruin the good creation and the people. It is domination—in this verse expressed as "rulers," "authorities," "cosmic powers," and "spiritual forces of evil in the heavenly places"—that deforms humans and human community. These powers reside in the "heavenly places"; that is, the powers claim to be the ultimate ideal for being human by claiming to be of divine origin.

When Jesus heals, he is fulfilling a part of the expectation of the messiah, yet he is also challenging the limitations of these expectations insofar as how, when, and who is healed. When Jesus eats with sinners, tax collectors, gentiles, and so forth, he likewise evokes these expectations, but he does so in a way that radically expands the list of who is invited to participate in God's reign.

When resisted by his Jewish and Roman contemporaries, Jesus refused to resort to violence. Further, he employed what we today call nonviolent means to raise issues, expose tensions, and change people's minds.

In stating that the kingdom was near us and among us rather than our possession, Jesus put a halt to the perfectionist dreams that usually lead to first, frustration with; next, anger at; and finally, violence against those who "don't get it."

In his nonviolent public leadership, Jesus was not simply another revolutionary; he was proposing a way to be human and humanity. His proposal entails our practicing baptismal awareness and participating in God's Reign of Mutuality rather than dominance and submission. He proposed that we work toward mutuality culture from within whatever culture we find ourselves.

Jesus was not naïve about the challenges and dangers involved in such apprenticeship.

CHAPTER EIGHT

Jesus' Third Way

Any high school history class can name countless cultures that have sanctioned terrible things in the name of goodness and virtue, espousing high ethical standards while breaking those same standards. The history class has the opportunity to see how the citizens of those cultures felt that theirs was the highest and best culture ever, and how the same citizens resisted knowledge of terrible acts, defending their culture against prophets who told them the truth about those terrors.

For the Jewish people of his day, Jesus was such a prophet. Ironically, some in our culture use Jesus as a defense against the prophets of our own day.

Why?

Let's use electricity as an image. If you touch copper wires carrying an electric charge, you are safe as long as there is insulation between you and the wires. Should you scrape off the insulation, however, you will receive a shock when you touch the wires.

When the prophet begins to uncover disturbing things about a culture, she or he is scratching off the insulation of culture. When this happens, people are forced to experience their true situation more directly. The prophet becomes the conduit though whom they experience the conflict between their desire for life and the reality of death. Because there is so much charge built up within them, this is quite difficult. They feel terror, and then they feel anger at feeling terrified. They often assume that the prophet, and not life itself, is the source of this terror. These feelings lead them to imagine the prophet as being the source of death. They often treat the prophet as they would an external enemy, such as a political terrorist. This is why we stone the prophets.

Any time a prophet attempts to tell the truth about a culture for the purpose of bringing about change, he or she is scraping off the insulation that culture provides its people. The danger for the prophet increases the more a culture is based on denial and domination. This is true, I imagine, for two reasons: 1) The more we deny our true situation, the more insulation we need to keep us from conscious awareness of it, and so the latent energy (repressed feelings) is greater within both individuals and the culture as a whole. 2) Domination cultures invariably call for a violent response to those who challenge their cultures.

When a prophet challenges a domination culture, its people respond with sudden and chilling ferocity. The psychologists who work with Terror Management Theory call this response "worldview defense." Prophets know that the high voltage of this defense could kill them. Prophets are often killed. Yet, even in death, these same prophets continue to be a source of inspiration and change.

The primary source of resistance to Jesus was the worldview defense of the Romans and their collaborators. We may imagine the only reason for resistance to Jesus by the collaborating Jewish leaders was that their jobs, privileges, or lives were on the line. Indeed, these powerful factors must not be underestimated! Nevertheless, I would argue that worldview defense is a deeper reason for their resistance.

To bring about change, you must challenge people's cultural insulation long enough and with enough intensity to get their attention. To bring such change nonviolently, you must be prepared to handle the high voltage your challenge will set free.

Again, when you challenge someone's cultural insulation, you are creating awareness in them of their own anxiety about death and limitation. No matter how kind your intentions, they will see you as a threat—not merely to some optional beliefs they hold, but to their very lives. Their long-repressed anxiety about death is set free in the instant you express a different view.

This explains why fundamentalists of any religious or cultural belief system respond so forcefully to those who espouse beliefs different from their own. Indeed, one could define fundamentalists as people so enmeshed in their cultural insulation to avoid death that they simply cannot question it. When their tightly held cultural insulation is questioned, they feel threatened with death and feel their anxiety about death full force. In their eyes, every different opinion carries with it the unconscious spectre of death, and even the nonviolent public leader will be seen as the very image of death, even the very source of death.

Possible Responses

When a prophet, or a prophetic movement, responds to violence with violence, he or she confirms a premise held by a culture of denial and domination and justifies its violent actions backwards in time. "You see, those people are dangerous," the initiator of the violence says. "We were right to use violence against them; it was a preemptive strike against those who were going to hurt us anyway."

When a prophet responds to violence with mere submission and fear, he or she also confirms a culture of denial and domination. Now the threatened culture can say, "We were right to use violence, because whereas they wanted to hurt us before, now we have made them too afraid to try."

Both of the above responses are what people generally expect in a culture of denial and domination. On the teeter-totter of dominance and submission, there are only two possible responses: fight or flight. When we act out of either dominance or submission, we are affirming the notion that denial and domination are necessary as the only framework in which human beings can live with one another—and since this is the only way, then it's better to be on top.

In an attempt to change this dynamic, Jesus chose a third response: He maintained his dignity and sense of power yet refused to resort to violence. By doing so, he confused his assailants. Maintaining his baptismal awareness and his vision that all are invited to live in God's Reign of Mutuality, he called into question his detractors' assessment of him and the possibilities in their relationship with him. He was strong and confident and remained so during and after each encounter with their violence towards him, and so did not confirm their use of violence against him. He called into question their assumption that the teeter-totter of denial and domination, with its latent store of violent energy, is the only way humans can live. He was committed to maintaining a mutual relationship with all of whom he came into contact, even his executioners.

Methods of Worldview Defense

People do not usually choose violence as their first weapon in resistance to change. It takes too much energy. They generally first try to dismiss, assimilate, or subvert; only after these tactics fail, do they move toward annihilation of the threat. Even a quick reading of the gospels reveals that Jesus encountered each of these strategies in resistance to the change he proposed. He gave fair warning to the students of his school of humanity that they would be likewise resisted "for that is what their ancestors did to the prophets."

Initially, the leaders within Jesus' culture tried to dismiss him. When he healed a man born blind, the Pharisees said, "You are his disciple, but we are disciples of Moses!" Fearing that Jesus was continuing to meet the people's expectations for the messiah (albeit in a surprising way), the leaders blindly sought to revile Jesus and the man who was healed. The gospel writers show one group after another trying to either dismiss him or set him up for an execution during the week before his arrest.

> So they watched him and sent spies who pretended to be honest, in order to trap him by what he said, so as to hand him over to the jurisdiction and authority of the governor. So they asked him, 'Teacher, we know that you are right in what you say and teach, and you show deference to no one, but teach the way of God in accordance with truth. Is it lawful for us to pay taxes to the emperor, or not?' But he perceived their craftiness and said to them, 'Show me a denarius. Whose head and whose title does it bear?' They said, 'The emperor's.' He said to them, 'Then give to the emperor the things that are the emperor's, and to God the things that are God's.' And they were not able in the presence of the people to trap him by what he said; and being amazed by his answer, they became silent. (Luke 20:20-26)

The leaders of the temple were held accountable to Rome for keeping their people in order. Not doing so could mean execution or, at minimum, removal from office. The strategy they had employed up to this time was dismissal of Jesus as crazy and unfaithful to their Jewish culture. During the Passover week, however, Jesus raised the stakes. He came into Jerusalem at a time when the city was swollen with potentially hundreds of thousands of pilgrims. Additionally, Pontius Pilate had arrived with legions of Roman soldiers to keep control over this celebration. Imagine the tension between an occupied and enslaved people celebrating a remembrance of being freed from slavery and the soldiers and other order-keepers who were keeping the celebrants enslaved!

In front of many people, the temple authorities put Jesus in what seemed to be a catch-22 situation by challenging him with a double-edged question: Is it lawful to pay taxes to the emperor or not? In response, Jesus asked them to produce the coin with which the tax was paid. While no idolatrous graven image was allowed in the temple, the authorities produced a coin on which Tiberius' image was probably engraved, along with the words, "Tiberius, divine son of the divine Augustus." In producing the coin with its forbidden image, Jesus' questioners had discredited themselves, exposing their collaboration with Rome. Jesus then answered simply: "Give to Caesar the things that are Caesar's, and to God the things that are God's." In speaking these words, he was not advocating for a separation of church and state; rather, as any young Jewish person could tell you, he was saying that everything belongs to God and nothing belongs to Caesar.

The strategy of dismissing Jesus having failed, they moved quickly to the end game.

> Now the chief priests and the whole council were looking for testimony against Jesus to put him to death; but they found none. For many gave false testimony against him, and their testimony did not agree. Some stood up and gave false testimony against him, saying, 'We heard him say, "I will destroy this temple that is made with hands, and in three days I will build another, not made with hands." ' But even on this point their testimony did not agree. Then the high priest stood up before them and asked Jesus, 'Have you no answer? What is it that they testify against you?' But he was silent and did not answer. Again the high priest asked him, 'Are you the Messiah, the Son of the Blessed One?' Jesus said, 'I am; and you will see the Son of Man seated at the right hand of the Power", and "coming with the clouds of heaven." 'Then the high priest tore his clothes and said, 'Why do we still need witnesses? You have heard his

blasphemy! What is your decision?' All of them condemned him as deserving death. Some began to spit on
him, to blindfold him, and to strike him, saying to him,
'Prophesy!' The guards also took him over and beat him.
(Mark 14:55-65)

Temple worship was considered unconditionally essential by the Jewish leadership of Jesus' day. For them, there was no other way to maintain
relationship with God but through the ceremonies and sacrifices that
took place on the temple grounds. Additionally, the temple symbolized
the strength and vitality of their culture—even though, in order to maintain temple worship, the chief priests had to play by the Roman rules. Jesus had undermined their power by forgiving and healing people without
temple sacrifice, by discrediting the authorities with the coin maneuver,
and by teaching the way of mutuality. The deeper issue, however, was that
Jesus was undermining their culture and therefore stripping away their
insulation. In so doing, he had exposed both the specific threat of the
Romans and the general threat of death.

In this passage from Mark, Jesus again uses the son of man title, referring to the character of God revealed in a free people of Israel, and the
character which he embodied. As such, the temple authorities saw him as
such a challenge to their culture, and to their insulation, that they sought
to annihilate him and his proposal for the way to be human.

Jesus' Choice for Nonviolence

Given the prevailing level of despair and anger at the Roman denial
and domination culture, in addition to the widespread belief that a military messiah would lead in battle against Rome, Jesus must have made a
conscious choice for nonviolent change. Many were collaborating with
Roman domination. Many had either fallen into submission to this
domination or were waiting for change to come from above. Given the
numbers of these debilitated people, Jesus must have made a conscious
choice for risky leadership and engagement with his culture.

Let's review: Jesus' command to take up his "cross daily and follow
me" has two major implications for how human beings live life and create
change.

First, in proposing a moment-by-moment baptismal awareness—that
is, being conscious of our vulnerability (symbolized by the cross) and

being affirmed by the Creator, which gives us courage to live life (symbolized by creation, resurrection, and recreation)—Jesus frees us to be more authentically who God made us to be. As we consciously feel the emotional implications of death and limitation, we have less dependency on our culture for affirmation. And if that culture is based on denial and domination, we become more able to relate to self, others, and our world from a heart that is more deeply joyous and playful.

Second, Jesus' call prepares us for the consequences of nonviolent public leadership in response to God's Reign of Mutuality. Baptismal awareness enables us to face the inevitable and potentially violent worldview defense of those seeking affirmation by a culture of domination as we live out the new humanity in their midst. When we sufficiently deal with the emotional consequences of death, we are less likely to be overwhelmed by the threat of force that would otherwise cause us to choose either retreat or violence. As we engage in nonviolent public leadership and are viewed as the threat of death, we are less likely to respond with violence or intimidation toward our detractors. We are able to view their threat to us realistically, for what it is, rather than as a conduit of our stored charge of denied death.

This increased emotional capacity to deal nonviolently with violent worldview defense is critical to our participation in God's catalytic reign. Culture is our way to avoid and distract ourselves from the emotional consequences of death. When our culture is challenged, humans tend to feel that death is somehow closer. Consequently, those who challenge our culture will be resisted in the most emotionally charged and violent ways. If they can respond in an emotionally balanced way—show no aggression and receive aggression without resorting to it—they have a chance to break the cycle of denial and domination.

Jesus' third way is living out God's Reign of Mutuality instead of the dominance and submission of the kingdom of domination. It supports active nonviolent leadership instead of collaboration, purity movements, separatism, violent revolution, denial, or passive resignation to the status quo.

The Lever for Change

As we challenge a community's insulation, we receive the energy that is built up beneath that insulation. Again, this energy is created by the tension of our situation: Humans desire life and we know we will die.

We seek affirmation from culture to insulate us from our situation. In tandem, we need to affirm the culture that affirms us. This leads to an intense and often violent worldview defense against any who would question our culture's ideals as being truly ideal. This is the primary source of danger for a prophet. It is why prophets are often killed.

This tandem need, to be affirmed by culture and to affirm culture, is also the prophet's primary lever for change.

Prophets use this lever in two ways: 1) by calling people to more faithfully live out the human ideal they already ascribe to, and 2) by challenging the society to a higher ideal. When a prophet, or a prophetic community, is able to maintain great enough tension and attention on how their culture is falling short of its own or a higher ideal, others within the culture are highly motivated to change.

Many who write about nonviolent change call this "moral force," yet they rarely offer an explanation for its capacity to create change. Even Martin Luther King, Jr. wrote that the "power of the nonviolent march is indeed a mystery."[35] It works because people need to feel that their culture is ideal in order to experience most fully the insulation it provides them. People are often willing to change when they see that 1) their culture is in fact not ideal, and 2) there is hope they will be able to bring about change. The trick is to get their attention, create tension, sustain the ethical argument, and maintain a calm, nonviolent stance. Additionally, when confronted by violence, the nonviolent leader embraces her or his vulnerability and power. This evokes, over time, a response of compassion even from those who perpetrated the violence. "Surely this man was the Son of God," said the centurion.

Jesus compared and contrasted the highest values represented in his Hebrew tradition with those values that were being lived out around him. In so doing, he issued a call to his Jewish brothers and sisters (as well as to the Roman hierarchy) to be honest about the fact that they were not living up the ideals they espoused. He also challenged his culture to question some of their ideals, measuring them by what might be considered more truly ideal.

In addition to the lever presented in cultural affirmation, a dynamic described in the psychological term, "projection," comes into play.

Example: A parent takes a three-year old to a new playground. The child feels vulnerable to this new, larger world. During this first visit to the playground, the child expresses the anxiety to his or her parent, asking the parent to bear it. The parent provides a lot of support to show that this world is safe for the child. The child's anxiety has been "projected" onto the parent. The second or third time the child approaches this playground, the wise parent steps back and waits for the child to enter the playground on his or her own. Now the child can enter into a larger world, having realized his or her own power to do so. An unskilled parent will continue to behave as though the child has no power and the world is too dangerous long after these fallacies have left the child's imagination. This parent will persist in providing uncalled-for support and, in so doing, risks creating an unhealthy dependency between child and parent.

Projection is temporarily necessary for any of us as we greet major change in our lives. The world is indeed bigger than we are. We are vulnerable and we need others to support us as we wriggle free from our comfortable layer of insulation to experience the world more honestly.

Negative Projection

Nonviolent leaders frequently become the object of trusting projection. They also become the object of projection of fear, anxiety, and hatred felt by the detractors of change. Having scratched off a layer of cultural insulation from a portion of the population, nonviolent leaders receive the full voltage of people's fears. It is critical that the change-leader be able to understand and respond well to this projection in both personal and public statements, as it offers detractors an opportunity to recognize that their perception of the leader, no matter how strong, may not be correct, and so become open to a new appraisal of the situation.

By not excluding from mutuality those who are participating in or perpetrating evil, nonviolent leadership makes change possible even in those who respond with negative projection. As Martin Luther King, Jr. wrote:

> The Negro must love the white man, because the white man needs his love to remove his tensions, insecurities, and fears. Agape is not a weak, passive love; it is love in action. Agape is love seeking to preserve and create community.[36]

Jesus met with a Pharisee named Nicodemus. He conversed and ate with Samaritans, healed a centurion's servant, and went to the country of the Geradens—a gentile community. He refused to believe the lie that "others" were his enemies. He was willing to accept both the positive and negative projections of the human beings around him. To those who tried to bully him, he responded without resorting to either violence or submission. To those who tried to reduce their own humanity by giving him power that belonged to them, he responded by lifting up their own responsibility and power.

How can a change-leader deal with the energy of death terror that lies beneath each human's cultural insulation? Through consciously dealing with his or her own desire for life and consciousness of mortality (baptismal awareness), such leaders increase their ability to recognize and handle this energy from others. We learn to process this energy and recognize it for what it is. Then, as others respond to the change we represent, they do not see their own fears reflected back at them. To quote the Proverbs, "A soft answer turns away wrath, but a harsh work stirs up anger." (Proverbs 15:1)

We have all seen how two angry people can reflect and amplify each other's anger until violence erupts. Learning to embrace our reality gives us the capacity to absorb and deflect, rather than reflect, so that we do not amplify the pent-up terror beneath another's cultural insulation. Their terror washes through us and goes to ground. At some point, this energy spends itself, and instead of seeing us as the very image and creator of death, they see a human brother or sister. As Bonhoeffer wrote:

> The only way to overcome evil is to let it run itself to a standstill because it does not find the resistance it is looking for. Resistance merely creates further evil and adds fuel to the flames. But when evil meets no opposition and encounters no obstacle but only patient endurance, its sting is drawn, and at last meets an opponent which is more than its match. . . . by willing endurance we cause suffering to pass. Evil becomes a spent force when we put up no resistance. By refusing to pay back the enemy with his own coin, and by preferring to suffer with resistance, the Christian exhibits the sinfulness of (violence and insult). Violence stands condemned by its failure to evoke counter-violence.[37]

Jesus was willing to accept the negative projection of a Jewish leadership that was captivated by domination and denial to the point where they felt they could do nothing less than annihilate the threat he represented by killing him. He believed that his death and his response to it would expose the truth about how human beings can live and would energize his apprentices to carry on after his death.

Positive Projection

Nonviolent leaders frequently become the object of trusting projection for many of those who would benefit from cultural change. Jesus, Mahatma Gandhi, Martin Luther King, Cesar Chavez, Dorothy Day, and many other agents of change have borne this form of projection from their supporters.

The problem with attempting leadership while bearing this type of projection is that leaders usually fall short of their own ideals, let alone the ideals of their admirers. King's reported affairs and Gandhi's strained relationship with his children led many to become disenchanted with their leadership. This is why both spoke of God as the real leader in this change toward a mutuality culture. The only object of projection that can stand up fully to the pressure is a God beyond our idea of God. King spoke of the "long arm of the universe swinging toward justice." Gandhi wrote that "The Indians' only weapon was a faith in the righteousness of their own cause and in God."[38]

Projecting our own power onto leaders of any mutuality movement can be only, at best, a step towards our participation in the larger world of God's reign. Saints and leaders themselves need to be deconstructed so that we do not get stuck and become dependent on them. Saints are, after all, just human beings. The instant we make them out to be more than human, we are already far down the path toward denial and domination, imagining ourselves as being subservient to them. (Of course, this posture would be comfortable for us.) If they are superhuman in some way, then the best we mere mortals can do is to quote them. In doing so, we can return to our comfort zone, having turned our exemplary way in into our easy way out.

Ultimately, the three-year-old needs to run into the park without holding her parent's hand. After this happens, the parent can enjoy play with her on a more equal footing. With our imagination set free by the example of these nonviolent leaders we are freed to engage in our own. This does not mean that the goal of nonviolent leadership is to be famous, however. The important thing is to engage in the kind of leadership, grounded in baptismal awareness, that is a joyful response to God's Reign of Mutuality.

No one person or group can single-handedly lead us in the sort of nonviolent cultural change I am describing. Against the forces on the ground and in the minds and hearts of every person, no one person or group can hope to prevail alone. To even attempt such a venture would be ludicrous. On the other hand, to participate and to do your part with others in what God is doing—that is possible!

This is the genius of Jesus inviting others to join him in the emerging and inbreaking reign of God.

> Very truly, I tell you, the one who believes in me will also do the works that I do and, in fact, will do greater works than these, because I am going to the Father. (John 14:12)

Jesus called his apprentices to join him in mutuality. Jesus' way of leadership takes us from enemies and strangers to full partners with him. When he sent his apprentices on a training mission without him, when he called them friends, when they experienced the presence of the Holy Spirit and were then sent into the streets, Jesus signaled that the goal of his leadership is full partnership with his apprentices.

Paul continued in this tradition when he said that the distributed gifts of the community lead us, as a community, to the full stature of Christ:

> The gifts he gave were that some would be apostles, some prophets, some evangelists, some pastors and teachers, to equip the saints for the work of ministry, for building up the body of Christ, until all of us come to the unity of the faith and of the knowledge of the Son of God, to maturity, to the measure of the full stature of Christ. (Ephesians 4:11-13)

We owe much to the late Murray Bowen, who pioneered Family Systems Theory.[39] He said that healthy leadership in any family, company, or society requires differentiated leaders. Differentiated leaders work hard to understand themselves, take clear positions, endeavor not to merely please others, and develop a capacity to decide how to relate to a person, no matter how the other initially responds. Jesus intends for his apprentices to engage in this kind of leadership, doing both the inner work of baptismal awareness and the outer work of nonviolent public leadership.

The Cross of Jesus

The consequences of Jesus' allegiance to God's Reign of Mutuality in the midst of the Roman Empire and its collaborating Jewish leaders were inevitably severe. Jesus called his apprentices and told them that to follow him was to daily take up their cross. This means to be conscious of their own mortality, limitedness, and vulnerability in each moment; to entertain the very real possibility of being killed for subversive activity; and to trust that God's promises to restore the world to wholeness would inexorably be realized. Jesus' apprentices were to take up his leadership in nonviolent cultural change and baptismal awareness in order to lead the world toward a new way of being human: living authentically and peacefully in the mutuality culture of the Reign of God.

We could then say that Jesus calls his apprentices to:

- join him in baptismal awareness;
- join God as God brings God's Reign of Mutuality;
- see the lie of denial and domination and its ideal of power;
- expect the resistance of both the dominators and the dominated;
- recognize our own limitedness and mortality every day, so that we can respond nonviolently and consciously to this resistance; and
- trust in the inevitability of the God's reign, and in the Creator's promise of resurrection.

Because he did not have to deny death, but daily dealt with its terror, he could live out God's vision of a world in which the sword and spear were turned into farming tools. Violence comes from the terror of death and our unconscious attempts to avoid it. Those who strive for consciousness of death and deal with the terror of our situation find that violence is not a reaction but rather a choice that one can reject.

Every day, Jesus courageously embraced the life that includes death. Every day, he died on a cross. Every day, he found affirmation from the God beyond our idea of God. This, again, is what I mean by baptismal awareness. When he was arrested and sentenced to death on the cross, he felt all the trepidation, pain, and horror that any of us would have felt. Yet because he had learned to face the reality of death each day, he was able to move through those feelings and ask God to forgive those who did not know what they were doing.

Jesus had long known the likely result of the kind of challenge his life and teaching represented. In the third of his statements about the response of his culture to the changes he proposed, Jesus said that "[He] will be mocked, and insulted and spat upon. After they have flogged him, they will kill him, and on the third day he will rise." (Luke 18:32-33)

The Resurrection of Jesus

Jesus believed in his resurrection. Remember the original context of resurrection: On the day of the messiah's victory, God would raise to new life the faithful remnant who had died while under the culture of denial and domination. It was a matter of God's justice and a promise for the new future made possible by God. Life is a good gift that is given again to human beings as a part of a restored creation.

Jesus was the first to believe in his resurrection. He believed that denial and domination are not the true character of God's universe. He believed that death is not a final word, rather that God's gift of life would ultimately bring death to death. He believed that God affirms our life with full knowledge of our death. Even so, this does not mean (as we so often re-interpret its meaning in our attempt to make Jesus into a tool of our own denial) that we can avoid our own feelings about our death and vulnerability. Jesus came to new life through death, not around it.

We come to new life that way, too.

When his apprentices experienced him raised from the dead, they looked about with transformed eyes and saw the world anew. In his death, they had faced their own; in his rising, they found a new way of life affirmed. In the power of the Spirit, they realized that they were indeed called and capable of continuing Jesus' work of living out the Reign of Mutuality in the midst of the Roman Empire, teaching the baptismal awareness, and inviting others into this new way to be human. They realized that they could take up their own experience of high-voltage human existence and learn to embrace it better. They now could risk following Jesus in both the daily spiritual practice of baptismal awareness and non-violent cultural change so that all might be free of the spell of denial and domination. They realized this new kind of life could handle the high voltage of being alive without requiring the constricting and deforming insulation of either the Roman or the Jewish domination culture. They were now free to grow as they would, no longer malformed by the social forces of domination.

They found that they shared a new worldview with one another.

Jesus and his apprentices understood that the method of holy war did not fit with the goal of a world of wholeness and peace. Violence nearly always leads to more violence, because most people choose to deny and repress their emotional response to death. Hence, any perceived threat to themselves immediately activates the vast pool of terror that lies, barely submerged, beneath the veneer of our every day lives. It is precisely *that* terror that begets violence. When we deal with that, violence will be defeated.

Jesus leads us to greater awareness of culture's life-destroying potential and teaches us to bring our death to consciousness daily. This makes his followers much less likely to "just react" to threat of violence. We are free to explore who God made us to be instead of needing to conform ourselves to prefabricated cultural roles. We no longer need to deny the reality of how our culture or country falls short of the ideal. Nor are we as likely to discharge the energy created by our true condition by abusing others, neglecting ourselves, or abusing drugs. Finally, because we are grounded in the ultimate affirmation of the Creator of the Universe, we are less likely to respond violently to those who are different.

To truly transform the world, one must bring people to consciousness of the terror of death while maintaining the deepest commitment to their well-being. Nevertheless, many people will regard any such attempt as a grave threat and react accordingly.

This brings us to another function of Jesus' call to take up our cross and follow him. Practicing baptismal awareness, we can consciously take up the supreme symbol of domination and expose it for what it is: a tool that taps into the powerful charge of terror that humans, denying death, have within them. Jesus accepted his death. He accepted his premature death as a likely consequence of his nonviolent public leadership. Jesus and his followers emptied the cross of its manipulative and controlling powers. Taking up their cross daily, they began a process of transforming the symbol of the cross from one of abject defeat to one of victory.

God's Response to Us

Jesus revealed how God would deal with human beings who live as powder kegs of unconscious fear. God would respond by suffering with them, accepting consciously what human beings deny and reject. Thus, God would give us another way, a third way, that exists beyond either seeking power like unto Caesar or passively accepting the degradation of slavery to Caesar.

Jesus is God's nonviolent response to us.

Many Christians resist this. We want God to be violent. Though Jesus' death and resurrection, God reveals that the Reign of Mutuality comes through nonviolent means. Some Christians, unwittingly serving as chaplains to domination culture in our time, propose that God needed Jesus' death so that God could forgive human beings. They seem to be saying that God requires punishment—or, more pointedly, that violence is a deep law[40] of the universe that even God cannot avoid. Ironically, they do not realize that this makes violence, not God, the ultimate god. God is not God if God's hands are tied. In doing so, they reveal that they are more attuned to the gods of Egypt, Babylon, and Rome than to the God of the Scriptures. We want God to be violent, not because of some respect for the Bible, but because we want God to bless the violence we participate in.

When we are captive to domination culture, God responds to us in Jesus: "Do what you will, I will not harm you. I will accept your violence without doing violence to you. I forgive you, for you do not know what you are doing. You seek to dominate others to avoid your own death, but your true fear is of your own creatureliness.[41] When you see that the Creator of the Universe accepts death in me and that I am raised from the dead, you will be invited to see things differently, give up your pseudo-heroic story, and join me in healing you and the world."

When we are captive to submission in denial and domination culture, God responds to us in Jesus: "I know what you are going through, for I have joined you. Death is a fearful thing, but I will face it with you. You have been oppressed by those seeking to repress their own fear, and you have been fearful yourself. I will help you face your fear and stand up as a human being, a child of the living God who continues to bring people out of slavery and into freedom. I will bring the world into wholeness, and I ask you to participate with me in its healing."

When we are captive to submission in denial and domination culture, God responds to us in Jesus: "I know what you are going through, for I have joined you. Death is a fearful thing, but I will face it with you. You have been oppressed by those seeking to repress their own fear, and you have been fearful yourself. I will help you face your fear and stand up as a human being, child of the living God who continues to bring people out of slavery and into freedom. I will bring the world into wholeness, and I ask you to participate with me in its healing".

In Jesus, God accepts our creatureliness—with its power and weakness, life and death, resiliency and vulnerability. He gets us out of the trap of sin, of rejecting life-as-it-is, falling into anxiety without trust, and living the teeter-totter of denial and domination.

God invites us to acknowledge our impossible situation, to feel the terror of it a little each day, and to trust in a God who suffers it with us and calls us to a more authentic ideal: participation in God's inbreaking and emerging Reign of Mutuality, trusting that God will bring the world to wholeness and will ultimately ensure our life.

Jesus responded nonviolently to the violence of the Roman Empire and the Roman-collaborating Jewish leaders who were attempting to protect their own culture. With his life and death, he revealed the true character and power of God—a Servant God who suffers with and for a hurting and incomplete creation and who seeks to make it whole. God suffers because the only way to respect the autonomy of human beings, and yet seek to heal them, is to suffer with them.

The deeper Biblical story reflected in Jesus' resurrection tells us that God intends to make a new heaven and a new earth—that is, a renewed imagination about God, the universe, and human beings, and healing to the earth and its peoples. This is the ultimate "end" of the universe, the goal toward which God is working, and the purpose of our apprenticeship.

When God completes the healing of the earth, God will raise all people from the dead, take them through a process of reconciliation, and live with them forever. Death is not the last word for God's sentient beings. Resurrection is. Hatred, fear, and war are not the last words for the human race. Restored relationship is. God asks us to love our enemies, yet God loves God's enemies until they are no longer enemies. The place where this happens is not in the clouds or in some heaven light-years away. The place is here, Planet Earth. We are living on Earth, and our job is to take part in the healing of the world until God completes this work. Earth is not disposable, but a cherished creation worthy of God's ongoing creative work.

A New Earth

For many people, the basic question posed by Christianity is "who gets to heaven and who goes to hell?" This notion of heaven and hell has functioned in an authoritarian manner much of the time. Domination culture has used heaven and hell as a way to promote a violent cosmos made by a law-and-order, authoritarian god. Domination's god sets up a universe in which some conscious creatures will inevitably exist in eternal torment. Domination's god is eternally violent toward people who do not believe or do certain things. Domination's god might want us to strive for heaven, but its notion of heaven means rejoicing there even as we know that others are suffering an unrelenting, eternal torture. Thus, domination's god is violent toward those in heaven as well as toward those in hell.

If the universe is essentially violent, then our violence toward those who are different from us is excused as a natural part of universal order. If God had set up an authoritarian universe, then we would feel right in doing the same. If God were to punish those who do wrong or who believe differently from us with eternal torture, then we, as agents of God, would feel justified in doing the same. If God were to use Earth as a lab experiment, then we would be given permission to treat it as resource to be used and spent, not a treasure to keep.

The god of which I write above is made in the image of domination to justify, promote, and mask domination culture's own ways. In worshiping this god, we are deformed and remade into the image of domination. This god tells us to obey the god-ordained governing authoritarians or face punishment now and after death.

We experience hell in many ways, but the God revealed in Jesus would not abandon anyone to it. We experience heaven in many ways, but the God revealed in Jesus would not subject us to a heaven marred by grief for abandoned loved ones. Jesus called his apprentices to love our enemies and do good to those who harm us. How could he call us to such actions when God does not do the same? No, it is domination culture itself that promotes this notion of a heaven-and-hell God to justify its own violence. This god is made in the image of domination; and through this deformed image, domination seeks to remake us in its own image.

Our God, revealed in Jesus, seeks the reconciliation of all things and all people. While this reconciliation is not yet complete, God will not stop until all the world is whole:

> For in him all the fullness of God was pleased to dwell, and through him God was pleased to reconcile to himself all things, whether on earth or in heaven, by making peace through the blood of his cross. (Colossians 1:19-20)

Defenders of the reward/punishment heaven and hell notion might say that people do terrible things, and a god who does not punish them is a permissive god who does not care for the victims of crime and violence. Indeed, a wholly permissive god would compromise the promise of healing and reconciliation as much as would an authoritarian one.

Still, there is nothing easy or painless about reconciliation. In the form of reconciliation that God intends in Jesus, the harsh truth of our destructive actions and attitudes are laid bare. The consequences of our actions are unrelentingly presented to us as we are led to engage those whom we have harmed. Some might call the pain of this reconciliation a "hell," but God's intent is to bring us to salvation—that is, to healing and wholeness. This will be a journey of pain and tears whose end is reconciliation with our identity as created in God's image—not in the image of domination, nor in the image of its counterpart, submission. God intends for all of God's creation to be brought to healing and wholeness—as individuals, healed and reconciled with our true selves and with our neighbors; as small communities, healed and reconciled with our larger, human community; and as humanity, healed and reconciled with all of creation.

In Jesus, God accepts our creatureliness—with its power and weakness, life and death, resiliency and vulnerability. He gets us out of the trap of sin: rejecting life-as-it-is, falling into anxiety because we are without trust, and living on the teeter-totter of denial and domination.

God invites us to acknowledge our impossible situation, to feel the terror of it a little each day, and to trust in a God who suffers it with us and calls us to a more authentic ideal: participation in God's inbreaking and emerging Reign of Mutuality, trusting that God will bring the world to wholeness and will ultimately ensure our life.

Jesus responded nonviolently to the violence of the Roman Empire and the collaborating Jewish leaders who were attempting to protect their own culture. With his life and death, he revealed the true character and power of God—a servant God who suffers with and for a hurting and incomplete creation and who seeks to make it whole. God suffers because the only way to respect the autonomy of human beings and yet seek to heal them is to suffer with them.

Risky Business

Jesus was clear that there would be casualties in such transformative work, yet that they, like him, would be raised from the dead and their risking-love vindicated by God.

> 'Blessed are those who are persecuted for righteousness' sake, for theirs is the kingdom of heaven. 'Blessed are you when people revile you and persecute you and utter all kinds of evil against you falsely on my account. Rejoice and be glad, for your reward is great in heaven, for in the same way they persecuted the prophets who were before you. (Matthew 5:10-12)

Jesus is not saying here, as some seem to suggest, that being persecuted makes one morally good. (Many wrongly assume they are fulfilling Jesus' words when, feeling threatened by religious differences, they act disrespectfully toward others and are understandably rejected for abusive behavior.) Jesus is saying that engagement in nonviolent public leadership brings the consequence of being resisted and persecuted—receiving the shock of worldview defense. As King said in his "I Have a Dream" speech:

> We must forever conduct our struggle on the high plane of dignity and discipline. We must not allow our creative protest to degenerate into physical violence. Again and again, we must rise to the majestic heights of meeting physical force with soul force. The marvelous new militancy which has engulfed the Negro community must not lead us to distrust of all white people, for many of our white brothers, as evidenced by their presence here today, have come to realize that their destiny is tied up with our destiny and their freedom is inextricably bound to our freedom. We cannot walk alone.[42]

Many say that nonviolence cannot work and dismiss it as a useless strategy. This is usually done without any logical assessment of the relative odds of success between violent and nonviolent means. Most of the time, this view is repeated almost as a statement of belief, as a central tenant of our culture's orthodoxy. Domination cultures insist that nonviolence does not work, as it makes us vulnerable to violence from others. It is, however, the fact of our vulnerability that is being rejected. In domination cultures we believe the lie that we can avoid our vulnerability through power over others. War is our most visible way of living out this lie—yet how many armed soldiers die in war? Nonviolence requires that we consciously embrace both our vulnerability and power. Not wanting to consciously acknowledge our vulnerability, we reflexively repeat the lie of our domination culture.

The method through which violence is unmasked is active nonviolence.

When Jesus actively responded without violence to the violence of the Roman Empire and its collaborators, he also revealed violence for the lie it is. In seeking to live out the Roman cultural ideal of power by killing Jesus, his assailants' insulation was doubly challenged, because 1) they knew he was innocent; and 2) therefore, as keepers of the cultural ideal, they were not living up to that ideal.

In Jesus, we see a God deep in the flesh of pleasures and pains, needs and strengths. He accepts what we reject: our mortality and limitedness. He does not stand against us, as do Pharaohs of every time with their ideal of power. Rather, Jesus stands with and among us, calling us to stand with him and resist domination and illusions of power that cause human beings and human societies to dominate others, ordering all things by arbitrary rankings of power and privilege.

Many see a contradiction between Jesus' claim that apprenticeship means both abundant life and risky nonviolent leadership that will likely include rejection and persecution. Some reduce "abundant life" to comfort while others reduce "risky leadership" to a death wish. Apprenticeship is the embrace of life-as-it-is that gives joy in life. This joyful embrace of life empowers our nonviolent leadership so that all may experience a more authentic life. Joy and love are the motivating factors for nonviolent leadership, not a death wish that seeks escape from life.

Nevertheless, most of us prefer denial and domination to baptismal awareness. The terror of our impossible situation makes us yearn for the dream of unlimited power, even though it is an illusion that brings more death and makes us agents of death.

> He sternly ordered and commanded them not to tell anyone, saying, "The Son of Man must undergo great suffering, and be rejected by the elders, chief priests, and scribes, and be killed, and on the third day be raised." Then he said to them all, "If any want to become my followers, let them deny themselves and take up their cross daily and follow me. For those who want to save their life will lose it, and those who lose their life for my sake will save it. What does it profit them if they gain the whole world, but lose or forfeit themselves? (Luke 9:21-25)

Jesus calls us to die, which is to enter into the consciousness of our death and mortality and see that God is there. He calls us to baptismal awareness, which is what he means when he says, "Those who want to save their life will lose it." We lose it because we are so fearful of death that we grasp life with such terror that we are unable to ever truly live. We give away life to avoid death. We reach out to whatever god of power we can find and cling to it even when it kills millions and crushes even ourselves. And when we see the effects of that crushing—the plight of the immigrant, the widow, the orphan, the AIDS victim, the homeless, and on and on—all we can say is, "Better them than us."

When the Pentagon smugly labeled the eminent bombing campaign on Baghdad as "Shock and Awe," their strategy was not only to shock the Iraqis (who live in the location of ancient Babylon, ironically enough) into feeling awe. The tactics employed in "Rapid Dominance" were meant to help achieve support at home by tapping into our need to feel powerful as citizens of a powerful country. Ironically, because of the powerful forces of worldview defense after the attacks of September 11, 2001, many felt powerless to even question the wisdom of the war.

This was not Jesus' way. He grew up in a tradition that, at its best, resisted Egyptian, Assyrian, Babylonian, and Roman domination. Jesus knew that the only way to live in the kingdom of God while living in the kingdom of domination was to be continually conscious of our death and limitation and to embrace our life as good—and, having done so, to then resist the culture of domination created by denial of our true situation. He called his apprentices to live "in" the worldview of domination but not "of" it.

How could he bear that? How could Jesus resist the whole of the Roman Empire and its client kings—who, in his case, happened to be Jewish?

Jesus was totally allegiant to a God who with power created all things, yet whose primary character is the willingness to suffer with and for us so that we can fully participate in God's love. That suffering love was revealed in the creation of the universe, whose nature transforms death into new life. That suffering love was revealed in the act of freeing the slaves from Egypt, who then had to die to their former lives in order to experience new life. It was revealed again when God returned the Israelites home from the Babylonian Exile and, again, new life was raised from the ashes of the old. That same suffering love was revealed not only in Jesus' death but also in raising Jesus from the dead, giving him new life and vindicating his way of living in the midst of a kingdom of death while being of God's Reign of Mutuality.

CHAPTER NINE

Apprenticeship Today

The church remained faithful to Jesus for many years, teaching and living out God's Reign of Mutuality. Early Christians practiced baptism and baptismal awareness. They believed they were living out the Reign of God in the midst of the empire and that, one day, the empire of domination and denial would fall and the earth and humanity would be restored.

They heard the call to come out of the ways of denial and domination and pledge allegiance to God's Reign of Mutuality.

> Then I heard another voice from heaven saying, 'Come out of her, my people, so that you do not take part in her sins, and so that you do not share in her plagues; for her sins are heaped high as heaven, and God has remembered her iniquities. Render to her as she herself has rendered, and repay her double for her deeds; mix a double draught for her in the cup she mixed. As she glorified herself and lived luxuriously, so give her a like measure of torment and grief. Since in her heart she says, "I rule as a queen; I am no widow, and I will never see grief", therefore her plagues will come in a single day—pestilence and mourning and famine—and she will be burned with fire; for mighty is the Lord God who judges her.' (Revelation 18:4-8)

As they "came out of her"—the Great Babylon that here symbolized the denial and domination of the Roman Empire—early Christians underwent a rigorous formation process that ranged from one to three years, during which they learned how to live in a new way *before* becoming a full member of the church. Baptism was the culmination of considerable study, prayer, and action. They gathered to remember that the world is lush and beautiful. They gathered to remember the resurrected Jesus as the source of life, and baptism as the way we re-enter the world—now seen as paradise.[43]

The early Christians followed Jesus in participating in nonviolent public leadership. Some of them paid the price of death for doing so. In 258 CE, Cyprian of Carthage (who talked about baptism as the reentry to paradise) wrote to some Christians who, enslaved to work in a mine, were chained and routinely beaten:

> Before being put in the mines you were beaten. But a wooden club does not frighten a Christian for our hope is in the wood of the cross. They chained you hand and foot, hurting you. But God is in you and you have courage—so your chains are not bonds but like bracelets made by the Lord. They will not let you wash yourselves, so that outwardly you are dirty, but inside you are pure and clean. You are cold because you don't have enough clothing, but the person who has "put on" Christ is well dressed. You cannot celebrate the offering of holy communion, but your lives are a precious offering and sacrifice, holy and acceptable to God, just as the apostle Paul wrote to the Christians at Rome.[44]

Later that year, Cyprian was arrested. Some of his friends and supporters begged him to escape, but he wanted to increase the tension between his ideals and those of the Roman governor who had sentenced him to death for not worshipping Roman gods. Because Cyprian had worked tirelessly during an epidemic to save people's lives, many citizens of Carthage were unhappy about both his sentence and his refusal to escape. After Cyprian was executed, Pontius the Deacon wrote:

> The date was September 14, 258. The place was Carthage. The emperor was Valerian, and the provincial governor was Galerius the Great. But the one who really has the power is our Lord Jesus Christ.[45]

For these and other early Christians, baptism was both a process and a ritual in which people became apprentices of Jesus—teachers and learners of baptismal awareness and risky participation in God's Reign of Mutuality. Baptism was a process of embracing the true condition of being human and coming out of the ways of domination.

> Do you not know that all of us who have been baptized into Christ Jesus were baptized into his death? Therefore we have been buried with him by baptism into death, so that, just as Christ was raised from the dead by the glory of the Father, so we too might walk in newness of life. For if we have been united with him in a death like his, we will certainly be united with him in a resurrection like his. We know that our old self was crucified with him so that the body of sin might be destroyed, and we might no longer be enslaved to sin. For whoever has died is freed from sin. But if we have died with Christ, we believe that we will also live with him. We know that Christ, being raised from the dead, will never die again; death no longer has dominion over him. The death he died, he died to sin, once for all; but the life he lives, he lives to God. So you also must consider yourselves dead to sin and alive to God in Christ Jesus. Therefore, do not let sin exercise dominion in your mortal bodies, to make you obey their passions. No longer present your members to sin as instruments of wickedness, but present yourselves to God as those who have been brought from death to life, and present your members to God as instruments of righteousness. For sin will have no dominion over you, since you are not under law but under grace. (Romans 6:3-14)

In baptism, Christians face our human mortality and limitedness. We experience death. Two elements are important here: 1) We face this with Christ, and 2) this leads to a new life in knowing God's embrace of our life. We do not walk this journey of learning to embrace our humanity alone; another has taken this journey before and meets us in the shadow of death. Yet this dark abyss, while all too true a part of the human experience, does not negate the value of our existence. Nor does death have the last word in our lives.

Having faced the darkness of mortality:

- We begin to experience a new life in which we embrace our own mortality yet find the affirmation of the Creator even so.
- We find a passion for living life arises from daily consciousness of our mortality and the daily gift of life, and we realize that each moment is a gift to be savored and to be grateful for.
- We can live the life that God has given us.

A similar reading could be made of the following verses so dear to the heart of the Lutheran tradition:

> But now, irrespective of law, the righteousness of God has been disclosed, and is attested by the law and the prophets, the righteousness of God through faith in Jesus Christ for all who believe. For there is no distinction, since all have sinned and fall short of the glory of God; they are now justified by his grace as a gift, through the redemption that is in Christ Jesus. (Romans 3:21-24)

The word "law" here refers not only to the 613 laws of the Torah that were being used in an oppressive way toward Jewish people in first-century Palestine but also to every cultural ideal. We are most susceptible to our culture when it is our only source of affirmation. Any set of ideals can makes us slaves in obedience to the denial and domination culture around us, but in Christ, we are liberated from the cultural ideals of domination through a free gift from God. The word "justification" was used in legal settings in Paul's day. Paul is saying that Jesus has released us from the court of public opinion, social pressure, and the cultural ideal of domination to live out a more truly human ideal. In baptismal awareness, we realize that we are justified by the God beyond our idea of god.

Justification of Being

Here, I want to address my Lutheran sisters and brothers for a moment.

For Lutherans, the concept of justification is central to understanding Jesus' ministry. Martin Luther was a Roman Catholic monk and a professor of Old Testament Theology. He struggled for many years with his worth as a person and his intense feelings of anxiety. As he studied the Bible in Greek, he realized that his worth was not based on what he did or did not do, but on God's free gift of love. In this free gift of love he gained some freedom with respect to his own culture. He found an affirmation that freed him from the ideals or works of his culture. In the passage from Romans shown above, he began to see that in Jesus' Christ we are "justified by grace through faith apart from works of law." In Jesus' death and resurrection we are given the gift of affirmation from God through a God-given trust. As the result of this affirmation that comes to us through trust, we are free to live in love for God, self, neighbor, and the world. In Lutheran circles, the words "grace" and "justification" are used to summarize this concept.

Unfortunately, many Lutherans have been taught that justification is primarily about alleviating our feelings of guilt—it is the means through which God forgives us. The idea of justification does include forgiveness and reconciliation with God and community at all levels of human existence. Indeed, the primary expression of anxiety about life and death in Luther's time was the feeling of mortality guilt, which the church both relieved and exploited. Luther's resistance to indulgences is witness to his concern about this. We frequently transform our fear of death and limitation into feelings of guilt in the way I did as a child. While receiving forgiveness can mollify our mortality guilt for a time, our comfort is short-lived, as this guilt provides a way to remain unconscious of the true source of our anxiety. While we are still vulnerable to anxiety expressing itself unconsciously as mortality guilt, this is not the primary or the only way Western people express anxiety today.

The common Lutheran proclamation of justification, however, often nostalgically hopes to mentally transport people into a pre-Reformation mind-set so that we can replay Luther's call to freedom without deeply engaging the specific word of grace needed in our particular time. This will not be met with a warm reception, as it is an answer to a question that few are asking.

The problem is that guilt is not the primary issue for individuals today: Death and our anxiety about it is. Today, justification by grace through faith means that God affirms our particular human life with its inevitable death and vulnerability. To Camus' question, justification by grace is the answer: It is the reason why not to commit suicide.

Trying to solve the problem of existence by offering grace centered on guilt traps us in passivity. We are told that we are forgiven by doing nothing, and so nothing is what we do. It is a good answer to the wrong question. Among many Lutherans, passivity is the new law, the new requirement, and we mistake it for the gospel. Justification is not about doing or not doing. It is about God's affirmation of our being and the freedom of the Christian from the constricting ideals of domination culture because of that affirmation.

Many times Lutherans use justification by grace as a way to distract people from their human anxiety. A person feels guilty. They are not sure why, but they desperately want the assurance of forgiveness, and so we tell them their sin is forgiven through God's grace. In this we are as much saying, "Don't explore this anxiety any further." We do not think to offer—with all the pastoral imagination we can muster—that their feeling of guilt is really their anxiety at being human, and that God's grace is really addressed to precisely that anxiety. We do not think to offer that in her or his existence with all its pains and joys, hopes and fears, she or he is affirmed by God and is now free to live that life joyously, embracing all of life's contradictions.

One is forced to wonder if Luther's understanding of justification and its address to our basic human anxiety is far deeper than most Lutherans have been prepared to consciously engage.

If Lutherans want to do more than merely recite Luther's words, we will need to delve more deeply into his writings, the writings of the church fathers, the creeds, the Scriptures, and the depths of our experiences. When we are faithful to the truth that Luther taught, we are drawn into freedom from domination culture and courageously post our own 95 theses—joining Luther in nonviolent leadership from within our own time.

Isaiah writes that we are arrows in the quiver of God. Many Lutherans refuse to be shot from the bow of God for fear of "works righteousness." If we do anything, then we will be in danger of not earning our relationship with God. This is a lie, albeit a tempting one. The arrow joyfully flies toward its target, having been set free by the power of the bow and the intent of its holder. Many Lutherans cling to the quiver and claim that our refusal of God's call is the very expression of our orthodoxy. Again, justification is an answer to the question of being; it is not about our doing or not doing. Attempting to avoid "works righteousness," we choose a passivity that is not evident in the life of Jesus, his disciples, Paul, or Luther.

Lutherans have fallen short of Luther. We have not dared go where Luther went, into the depths of despair and anxiety that he so obviously engaged, to find there the acceptance and embrace of God. We have failed to grasp that the freedom of the Christian is to be joyously expressed through action because it is the gift of God.

Additionally, because our existence is justified, we are free to look at the ways in which our lives fall short of the full stature of Christ. We are free to enter into deep repentance of how we have accommodated ourselves to domination. Repentance is not feeling bad, but changing our ways. We are free to question how the ways we live in community fall short of mutuality.

> Do not be conformed to this world, but be transformed
> by the renewing of your minds, so that you may discern
> what is the will of God—what is good and acceptable
> and perfect. (Romans 12:2-3)

Some Lutherans claim that the reason our churches are in numerical decline is because the culture just doesn't understand us and the truth to which we cling. It is not our countercultural message that has kept others from hearing the voice of our tradition (although sometimes our self-righteousness about it may play a part). It is our own refusal to enter deeply into the tradition that helped to form Luther's courageous life and express that in ways the culture can understand. We are called to go deep and go out.

Our focus on our numerical decline belies an even deeper issue: We measure the church by typical business standards, as if the church existed for itself, as if our mission was to survive or succeed. The church as Jesus envisioned it exists for the healing of the world, the creation, and human cultures. No vision short of this can legitimately be called Christian.

So, while Lutherans talk of the freedom of the Christian, few are freed up enough to move at all. Instead, many of our congregations merely represent a kinder, gentler version of the civil religion that is most of Christianity today.

Domination Baptizes Christianity

In 70 CE, in response to a violent Jewish revolution, the Romans destroyed the Jewish temple. An estimated 1,000,000 Jews were either killed or sold into slavery by the time the war had ended, and the remaining Jews were forbidden to come within sight of Jerusalem. This led to a cultural transition, the power of which has been often underestimated.

Within 70 years of its beginning, Christianity was no longer a Jewish sect led by people with intimate knowledge of Jewish culture, religion, and politics—as it had been in first-century Palestine. By the end of that century, Christianity was adapting to the culture of the Greeks and Romans. The longing of the Jewish people for liberation from Roman occupation by a messiah as the context for Jesus' own messiahship was lost in translation. Much of the language of the writings that became the Christian Scriptures is highly nuanced and playfully reinterprets Jewish expectations. When severed from their own time and setting, these writings became more difficult to understand and human beings began to reinterpret them in light of their own culture and needs. Certainly, these writings were always open to multiple interpretation. However, when the subtle cultural references are lost, it becomes very difficult to know if an interpretation is inside the ball park, so to speak.

The sad fact is that the Christian message became so severed from the context in and culture to which it was spoken that it became more difficult to discern the heart of the faith.

The acculturation of the Christian message to meet the needs of the Roman and Greek culture intensified dramatically when Constantine adopted Christianity as a state religion. Constantine's mother was a Christian. By some accounts, Constantine wanted Christianity to strengthen an empire weakened by plagues, wars, fires, and infanticide, and so he invited theologians and bishops of the churches to systematize a diverse Christianity. By other accounts, he wanted to subvert a movement that had become too large to control by any other means.

While the theologians and bishops of the church tried to make a faithful Christian response to the Greek and Roman cultures, they totally underestimated the power of the Roman domination culture. Until this time, Christian communities had often required years of formative education and training before a person could enter the church—needed because Christianity was understood to be an alternative culture that resided within yet worked to actively transform the domination culture. Becoming a Christian required a complete switch of allegiance. The theologians and bishops of the church tried to express the message of Jesus when the wrote the Nicene Creed, but they did so with the language of Rome and the philosophical concepts of Plato. Whereas Christian baptism prior to Constantine signified a switch of allegiance from Caesar to Jesus, Christianity itself was now baptized by Greek and Roman culture.

After Constantine's baptism of Christianity, Jesus' messianic community became mere Christianity. Enemy generals were baptized just before their beheading so they would "go to heaven" after they were executed. Millions were baptized with no formation whatsoever. Worship became a large-scale public event with little or no mutual relationship. The Constantinian Empire used Christian missionaries to soften up new territories for conquest. Constantine himself was not baptized until he lay on his deathbed. The messages implicit were powerful:

- Christianity was a way to support the Empire, not to overturn domination itself.
- Baptism was a way to deny the emotional consequences death by promising a better life after life was over.
- The baptism of an individual was a way to ensure and bless the status quo of domination as ordained by God.

So Christianity largely remains until this day—a tool of the powers that be. Christianity, as most of us experience it, is used in the same way as the ma'at of the Egyptians and the creation stories of the Babylonians. Originally, the title Son of God was in part used in reference to Jesus as a counter-claim to Augustus Caesar's the son of god title. Ironically, now Jesus as the Son of God was being used to bless another Caesar. When leaders in our time claim to be "born again," they are usually making essentially the same claim to divine approval as did Augustus Caesar. When many claim that America is a "Christian nation," they are seeking to define Christianity by their authoritarian vision of America and vice versa.

Where dismissal and annihilation had failed, incorporation and assimilation have succeeded. Almost. The alternative tradition that began along the Nile has always been a minority tradition. It has always been resisted. Yet, prophets and teachers worked to call their people back to the

God's way to be human and humanity. In the early fourth century, Jesus' community faced the challenge of assimilation by Empire. Yet since those times a faithful remnant has reminded us of God's vision for our world.

Dietrich Bonhoeffer bore witness to Jesus' vision of humans and humanity in the midst of a Nazi regime that nationalized Christianity as a propaganda tool. He wrote that Jesus' call to daily dealing with death and limitation is part of a joyous and faithful life. Bonhoeffer maintained that nonviolent public leadership is the way of Jesus and the way of a faithful apprentice.

> The followers of Christ have been called to peace.... And they must not only have peace but make it. And to that end they renounce all violence and tumult. In the cause of Christ nothing is to be gained by such methods....His disciples keep the peace by choosing to endure suffering themselves rather than inflict it on others. They maintain fellowship where others would break it off. They renounce hatred and wrong. In so doing, they overcome evil with good, and establish the peace of God in the midst of a world of war and hate.[46]

Any real hope for the human race depends on our ability to embrace the reality of our human existence and our choice to participate in mutuality culture. The future of the human race must include consciousness of the fact that culture, while good and necessary, has deep vulnerabilities that cause untold death and destruction.

The Problem and Promise of Religion

Douglas John Hall begins his book, *The Cross in Our Context*, with a haunting image. After the terrorist attacks leveled on September 11, 2001, someone wrote "Religion Kills" on the walls of a seminary in Montreal. Any apprenticeship of Jesus must take the dangerous potential of religion as a serious matter.[47]

The destructive power of social forces on human beings has been noted in the activities of Christians on numerous occasions throughout church history. Some well-known authors reject that the Christian tradition has any resources with which to wrestle with these issues. Many assert that no religion is of any use and that religion inevitably leads to violence. I understand their viewpoint, but I do not share it. If we were to throw away everything that has been used to foment violence, not much would be left to make peace. Indeed, to rid ourselves of everything useful in violence, we would need to do away with language itself!

We can honor the willingness of these writers to act as prophets. We can honor the deep love for humans that resonates in the pages of their books. However, in their analysis of our situation, they have not perceived the heart of the issue. Every religion on Earth has at times participated in the destructive forces of its culture. Religious leaders have very often supported the status quo of domination culture. Yet this is true of nearly all forms of leadership and institutions in cultures everywhere.

Religion itself is not the problem; the nature of human life and our response to that life is the problem. To think otherwise is an attempt to avoid the fact of our mortality and our commonly woeful response to it. It is only another attempt at denial—in this case, through scapegoating religion and the religious.

A Muted Word

Religion can easily embody not the risking-love of Jesus, but a false prophet for maladaptive culture. The church often does this by saying nothing at all, or by saying it so carefully it can be overlooked.

During the lead-up to the Iraq war, I took a vacation. I went to a church one Sunday and heard this: "Jesus teaches us the way of peace, and while our leaders may fall short of peace, we can always trust that Jesus will love us the way we are." Couched this way, the sentiment of the preacher (our leaders may fall short of peace) needed only be noticed by those who agreed with it. They quietly approached the preacher after worship and, with shining eyes, praised his courage. Those who disagreed or who thought the church should not have such conversations pretended to have dozed off during that part of the sermon. They passed to the exit door with the normal blessing of "Good sermon, Pastor." Many preachers do speak a prophetic word but speak the truth in a short phrase safely protected in the bunker of a compound sentence. These are "prophets for a phrase."

Dr. Martin Luther King, Jr., in his "Letter from the Birmingham City Jail," lamented the powerlessness and ineffectuality of the church.

The contemporary church is often a weak, ineffectual

voice with an uncertain sound. It is often the arch-sup-
porter of the status quo. Far from being disturbed by
the presence of the church, the power structure of the
average community is consoled by the church's silent
and often vocal sanction of things as they are.[48]

King and the movement he and others created strove to embody the
power of ancient faith traditions to challenge that same status quo with
courage and love.

Bonhoeffer gathered with other pastors and Christians to participate
in resistance. They spoke out against the use of God and Jesus to promote
Nazi ideals which condoned racism and murder of Jews and Romani. He
was killed in a German prison five days before its liberation by the U.S.

Christianity stands or falls with its revolutionary protest
against violence, arbitrariness and pride of power with
its plea for the weak. Christians are doing too little to
make these points clear rather than too much. Christen-
dom adjusts itself far too easily to the worship of power.
Christians should give more offense, shock the world far
more, than they are doing now. Christians should take
a stronger stand in favor of the weak rather than con-
sidering first the possible right of the strong. (Dietrich
Bonhoeffer, Sermon on 2 Corinthians 12:9)

Karl Barth, too, resisted the Nazi Party in Germany—until he was
expelled from the country. This long but worthwhile quote is his reflection on the often ineffective efforts within the church to oppose Hitler.

What we have to do is to say in common language of the
world the same thing as we say in the forms of Church
language. . . . We know this language of the pulpit and
the altar, which outside of the area of the church is as
effectual as Chinese. Let us beware of remaining stuck
where we are and refusing to advance to meet worldly
attitudes. In 1933 in Germany there was plenty of serious, profound, and living Christianity and confession—
praise be God and thanked! But unfortunately this faith
and confession of the German Church remained embedded in the language of the church, and did not translate
what was being excellently said in the language of the
church into the political attitude demanded at the time;

in which it would have to become clear that the Evangel-
ical Church had to say "No" to National Socialism, "No"
from its very roots. . . . May every individual Christian
be clear that so long as faith is a snail's shell, in which he
feels comfortable, but which does not bother itself with
the life of his people has not yet come to believe! This
snail's shell is not a desirable residence.[49]

Barth recognized that for many faith in Jesus can easily be turned into
a snail's shell, mere cultural insulation that serves to keep us comfortable
while the world is destroyed. This kind of faith is not really faith at all, he
says, for the person with this kind of faith "has not yet come to believe."
Not having grappled with life and death, this person uses their system
of religious beliefs to claim God's support their slavery to the status quo.

Bonhoeffer said much the same thing when he wrote about what he
called "cheap grace" in 1937. Cheap grace is the bland support of the
church for its host culture. Cheap grace is the forgiveness of those who
reside within their less-than-ideal cultural insulation as a means to excuse
them from the ideal of Jesus.

On the first page of *The Cost of Discipleship* he wrote:

Cheap grace means the justification of the sin without
the justification of the sinner. Grace alone does everything, they say, and so everything can remain as it was
before. 'All for sin could not atone.' The world goes on
in the same old way, and we are still sinners 'even in the
best of life' as Luther said. Well, then, let the Christians
live like the rest of the world, let him model himself on
the world's standards in every sphere of life, and not
presumptuously aspire to live a different life under grace
from his old life under sin.[50]

In the Bible, "world" and "flesh" are often used not to refer to the creation and our bodies, but to the worldview of domination. Bonhoeffer's
point, I think, is made clearer when we substitute the word "culture" for
"world." Let's read it again with that change:

Well, then, let the Christian live like the rest of the culture, let him model himself on the culture's standards in
every sphere of life, and not presumptuously aspire to
live a different life under grace from his old life under
sin.

Cheap grace simply affirms whatever culture it is in. It is the church as cheerleader for the perpetrators of genocide, as was so much of the church in Nazi Germany. Cheap grace has been the message of the church while a quarter-billion people have been murdered in genocide, transforming us into murderers, either passive or active.

Constantine's Cheerleader

The Christian church has played the role of cheerleader for the powerful since Constantine. The church has failed to take on the political powers and the culture of the day. It has failed to play its role in the development of a new humanity as a mutuality culture. It has failed to play its part in leading humanity in being human in the way proposed by Jesus. Rather than helping human beings to embrace our mortality and possibility, it has encouraged the spirituality of guilt. The church has taught that the high voltage of human existence—desiring life and being conscious of death—can be dealt with by feeling guilt instead of by practicing baptismal awareness. Every week, church-goers have been encouraged to release a little of the steam from this pressure cooker of guilt as we attended worship. We have been encouraged to see ourselves as despicable creatures and the church as that which would offer escape from our unmentionable condition. This version of the church did not name sin, but participated in and benefitted from it. When the church uses guilt in this way it is practicing a form of exploitation.

If sin is rejecting life-as-it-is so as to avoid our fear of death and the reality that includes death, then the church has often blessed sin in the name of Jesus and then rejoiced at the cash in the offering. Many theologians and pastors preach of the total depravity of the human being. In doing so, they appear to be taking sin seriously. When they preach this way and people encounter their desperate need for affirmation by the Eternal One, then, perhaps, it is excusable. Perhaps. But all too often this sort of preaching regresses to an argument for authoritarian rule and rules and, as such, contributes to the denial and domination of our time. All too often, this teaching is just another form of ma'at. All too often, this kind of teaching is not a fearless description of sin, but an expression of it. Despising life is not a way to express gratitude for life to the Author of Life.

Christians often respond to the "total depravity" argument, sometimes referred to as original sin, with the notion that human beings are originally blessed. Even as total depravity ignores our capacity for generosity, self-sacrifice, compassion and love, original blessing can ignore our capacity for violence and destruction. Original blessing, or the notion that people are "totally good," can too easily bless not only peaceable ways but also merely stable ones—saying "peace" when there is no peace.

"Total depravity" and "total goodness" are not the best terms to use, and their use reflects human sin. Taken alone, each makes a claim of an absolute truth about the universe and human beings. Total depravity implies that the world is a Lord-of-the-Flies world and we need authoritarian controls to keep the inmates under control. This argument rejects life-as-it is by despising humans. Total goodness implies that this world is the best of all possible worlds and that we can ignore its complexity and our complicity in the evils we do as well as those done on our behalf. It often expresses a grace that is deplorably cheap, blindly blessing the status quo of domination. This argument rejects life-as-it is by not coming to terms with it.

Scriptural writers paint a picture of a good, very good world that includes limits, vulnerability, and death—a world that we reject at gut level. In that rejection, we experience God's gift of a blessed life as a curse.

Scandal of the Cross

In 325 CE, early in Constantine's move to take over Christianity, he called together church leaders to produce a creed to describe the central teachings of Christianity at Nicea. The Council members did not intend to add fuel to our rejection of life when writing the Nicene Creed. Contrary to Roman culture, the Creed essentially states that the universe is the intentional creation of a God who declared it good, very good. The writers of the Creed tried to say that the earth is worth dying for. They tried to say that world continues to be a location of God's ongoing creativity and love and that it one day will be healed fully.

They tried to communicate, within a fourth-century Roman culture, that the scandal of the cross is the scandal of human existence, and if being human is good enough for God, it is good enough for us.

This message has been largely lost. Jesus' cross, instead of being seen as the primary revelation of the character of God, was turned into a dirty job that Jesus had to do so that he could go back to being in power— and not just any power, but power essentially no different from that of

Pharaoh, Caesar, and the rest. Not long after Christianity's baptism by the empire, Jesus was seen as the one who blessed the empire and the emperor—who, if not divine, had a divine right.

When we don't have a king, we enthrone our country as the best. Christian churches, in the words of Douglas John Hall, have supported the official optimism of North American culture. Beneath this official optimism is deep despair.

> Yet the demand for immediate (defensive) hope cloaks a far deeper, if less frequently verbalized need. Liberal and moderate Christianity in North America has so capitulated to the surface demands of its middle-class clientele that it is blind to the profound if usually unspoken yearning of the same middle-class. Quietly desperate people ask for a veneer of hope because they are deeply skeptical about the possibility of any other kind. If they could believe that there are grounds for a "hope that does not disappoint us," few would be satisfied with exhortations to a programmed cheerfulness and other solemn religious versions of the official optimism.[51]

Hall's words speak to the deep question for humanity in our time: What is the basis of our hope for the human race when hope has so often proven futile?

Leading as Jesus Led

Clearly, any individual or community that claims to be Christian needs to attempt to do what Jesus did. We are called to be apprentices, not groupies! An apprentice of Jesus is called to *practice* baptismal awareness, not to perfectly master it. Jesus does not demand that we be perfect in our attempts. Unless we know that God's love for us, as we are, is secure and deeper than life and death, we could not even attempt the practice of baptismal awareness.

Jesus embraced the reality of human existence with courage. He embraced this condition through spiritual practice: forty days of fasting in the desert, frequent times devoted solely to prayer within a life of continual prayer, and deep study of his faith tradition.

Jesus saw that the Roman and Jewish religious and political leaders of his time were living out of an ideal that was not life-giving. He was free to respond authentically, without fearing attack from those who did not approve of his view, his words, or his actions. Because he had faced his own mortality, he was able to be in, but not of, the maladaptive domination culture of his day.

While honest, it is painful to admit that much of the Christian church has failed to engage both our impossible situation and the nonviolent change that Jesus inspired. However, Jesus' strategy of transforming culture from within does not require that the church be perfect in the past, present, or future. Nor does it require that our host culture be perfect. The Holy Spirit continues to call all of us to come out of domination. God continues to overturn domination that we may learn to be more honestly and truly human. God calls us toward living out mutuality from within whatever culture we find ourselves in.

Yet we cannot participate in the healing of the world if we have not begun to participate in it ourselves. One of the potential dangers of this perspective is that it could be reduced to mere activism. Instead of joyously participating as vulnerable and powerful creatures in God's inbreaking and emerging reign, one could easily start on a never-ending quest to remake the world in our own image in order to find affirmation in being right. This sort of activism, without spiritual grounding, has the potential of becoming just another form of domination, just another set of cultural rules, just another kind of competition for power.

Baptismal awareness shows us that we don't have to be busy 24/7/365 on Kingdom business. We are freed from the cultural expectations that have haunted us—including ecclesiastical ones. This awareness can remind us that while the scope of God's healing is immense, we are called only to do our own part in partnership with others and, ultimately, in partnership with the Creator of the universe. Baptismal awareness might suggest that one part of the leadership we are being called is practicing times of joyful uselessness—that is, practice of the Sabbath.

Jesus, the gospels tell us, was an observant Jew who observed the Sabbath. He also took time away from his apprentices and the crowds for prayer and rest. Part of our leadership in a world busy to the point of exhaustion will be the gift of rest, enjoyment, and relationship.

Deep enjoyment is, after all, the purpose of creation. We are not perpetual ministry machines trapped in an endless, Sisyphean struggle to heal the world.

Jesus grew tired. He slept. He ate. He laughed and he wept. He looked at the sunset and pondered the stars. He did not accomplish the full healing of the world, but he was willing to die to begin it. If this life is good enough for him, then it is good enough for us.

Baptismal awareness and participation in God's Reign of Mutuality leads us out of the worldview of productivity, consumption, and perfection.

We are learning to embrace life-as-it-is. We are learning to enjoy life, to savor it as Jesus did and as God does.

Lastly, the leadership we are called to provide may in fact teach us how to risk and embrace our failures. When we risk participation in God's Reign, we will often not see any tangible results. Failure, too, is embraced and affirmed by God, and so it can be a source of laughter and learning .We know how the story ends, and so we can relax when a chapter does not go as we had planned.

Catechesis

The spiritual disciplines of the church now can take their proper place as part of baptismal awareness. They include ways of claiming time in our lives for recreation, meditation, reflection, and dancing in the beauty of life. These spiritual disciplines offer ways to explore an alternative worldview of mutuality. Not tasks to accomplish, they hold joyous methods of remembering and aligning ourselves with the true character of the universe.

The key spiritual discipline of the Christian church for our day is catechesis, the ancient practice of Christian formation. The word literally means "to sound down" or instruct. Catechesis was a one-to-three-year process in which prospective Christians changed allegiance from the kingdom of domination to the allegiance to God's Reign of Mutuality. This process culminated in baptism. Baptism represents entrance into and dedication to a way of life that includes a process for consciously embracing life-as-it-is while being committed to God's redemption of all people and all things. After Constantine's baptism of the church, catechesis was reduced in purpose, intensity, duration, and clarity about Jesus' mission. There are many in the church today who think we are in a multi-generational process of recovery from domination's subversion of Christ.

I envision a catechetical process of three years that the church and church members continually practice. Prospective members would go through their first cycle with the guidance and support of mature practitioners of baptismal awareness and God's Reign of Mutuality, yet all would remain practitioners, not masters.

To recover the distinctive worldview of baptismal awareness and God's Reign of Mutuality, it may be necessary to set aside infant baptism for a time. While this ancient practice is both biblical and sound, in our context it implies no switch of allegiance, no change of heart, no opened eyes. Many see it as a call to good citizenship, but not necessarily citizenship in God's reign. The alternative is to become much more clear about the role of sponsors and parents following infant baptism and the role of worship as a part formation for leadership in the world, and to cease the soft-selling of Christianity that we use in place of a real confirmation process. This is a discussion that the church needs to have.

Participants in a catechetical church need to continue to practice simple service and study of Scripture and tradition, employing reason and experience as partners in that study. A catechetical church needs to employ the art of discernment, both in its practice of exploring its own life and calling and in preparation for baptism or reaffirmation of our baptismal vows:

- to live among God's faithful people
- to hear God's word and share in Christ's supper
- to proclaim the good news of God in Christ through word and deed
- to serve all people, following the example of our Lord Jesus
- to strive for justice and peace in all the earth, and respect the dignity of every human being

The ongoing catechesis of the community needs to include many other spiritual disciplines and practices. Key among these is the Eucharist—the celebration of Christ's presence in the meal of bread and wine. The Eucharist is a meal in which we remember Jesus' death and resurrection as well as our own frailty as creatures who must eat to survive. In the act of eating and drinking together, we realize that we, such frail creatures, are given enough and an abundance—enough to share. In the Eucharist, we practice the great banquet of God's healing and thus practice the truest nature of the universe.

On this mountain the Lord of hosts will make for all peoples a feast of rich food, a feast of well-matured wines, of rich food filled with marrow, of well-matured wines strained clear. And he will destroy on this mountain the shroud that is cast over all peoples, the sheet that is spread over all nations, he will swallow up death for ever. Then the Lord God will wipe away the tears from all faces, and the disgrace of his people he will take away from all the earth, for the Lord has spoken. (Isaiah 25:6-10)

The very act of prayer, offered by a creature both frail and strong, can now be seen as conscious dependency on God and an act of imagining and affirming the kingdom of God.

Communal worship as a part of a community takes place in being grounded in the narrative of a God who is a nonviolent leader in the world, a serving God in whose image we are made.

Fasting can now be seen as an activity that reminds us of our own reliance upon food for survival. It offers the opportunity to strengthen and enhance our consciousness of mortality and limitation, and it fosters our growth in compassion for ourselves and for all life.

Calling and discernment in ministry can now be seen as an attempt to reveal our truest calling and identity. Discernment is tempered with the wisdom that tells us that, while each individual has incredible God-given power, no one person has all gifts and no one person has endless energy.

The Practice of Worldview Critique

Jesus invites his church into deep reflection on our culture, its promise, and its problems. This does not mean that we can claim to know what is best for all and that all other viewpoints are wrong. We are called only to deeply engage our culture from a perspective that is, at minimum, not wholly captivated by it. Answering Jesus' call to join him in God's Reign of Mutuality includes acknowledging that our current culture, no matter how well thought-out or how well lived, is not as fully ideal as it will yet be.

Jesus invites his church to think deeply in ethical reflection about the truth of the way we live and exercise our freedom in God's embrace. Here, ethical reflection involves deliberate thoughtful exploration and discernment of what it might mean to live out God's Reign of Mutuality in everyday life.

When I engage people in conversation concerning the Bible, economic issues evoke the highest emotions and resistance. Luther said that our god is whatever we fear, love, and trust. Our reaction to even basic conversation about economics reveals what our god, our idol is.

Domination is like a viral contagion that spreads from one host to another. We are profoundly susceptible to the teeter-totter of denial and domination because of the painful contradictions inherent to human existence. We tend to be very good at identifying historic expressions of domination and not so good at seeing those in which we participate. It is indeed a difficult shell game to beat. Many see the U.S. as the current preeminent domination system in the world. One can easily view our military use and spending as example of a domination culture at work. And while we are used to thinking of domination systems as forms of governance akin to those of the modern nation-state, not so readily apparent is the domination system at work in multinational corporations and the über-wealthy who control them.

One might say our modern-day über-wealthy—unlike Pharaoh, Caesar, and even our political leaders—do not openly promote their vision of the world. Modern social forces generally work more or less covertly, nearly invisible to the people whose lives they influence. In 2011, one only need ask who owns our media. Today, electronic media is the only way many of us get "information" about our world. Electronic media is today's church, cultural storyteller, imperial herald, and best friend for many of us. This media teaches us of a dangerous world, where chaos rules and where hope is gone. After so many mergers, this cultural storyteller increasingly speaks with one voice—at least, on most economic issues.

Out of the corner of our eyes, however, can we not see that capitalism has become our idol? Our cultural storytellers say that capitalism, not God, provides our food and comforts. They propose that "free capitalism" will provide even more. (We like the word "free.") They say that if government is fettering capitalism then we have to tear government down, because it limits the freedom of capitalism. (We don't like the word "limit.") They go on to say that it is government programs for the poor that are the source of our problems. Then, these Pharisees of capitalism say that the poor themselves are responsible for our troubled economy—they are "sinners" who could join us in getting rich if they only wanted to. They say that the jobs have moved to third-world countries because workers in first-world countries have asked for too much. (Ironically, our cultural storytellers are paid in the millions per year, but the über-wealthy do not seem to mind the high cost of marketing their story. It's simply the price one pays for anonymity while powerfully influencing the cultural story. (In previous centuries, many church leaders were bought off in the same way.)

These are but a few of the arguments furthered by the media controlled by the über-wealthy. These arguments are echoed frequently whenever people engage in discussion about Jesus and economics. Free market economics seems to have become the new orthodoxy, the new vision of being human and humanity. To be fully human is to be wealthy and powerful, to have white teeth and wear chic clothes–and only capitalism can make this possible. To be the ideal society, we must constantly increase our wealth and consumption of resources. To acknowledge the fact that we live on a planet of limited resources, that our use of fossil fuels is leading to global climate change, and that oil production has or is nearing its peak is considered heresy.

Our fantasy of unlimited growth is nothing more than an expression of our search for power and denial that we are limited, mortal creatures living on a limited, mortal planet. Capitalism is the new ma'at, the divine order given by God. Today, we experience a multinational, corporate Babylon.

After the rise of the Nazi Party in Germany, Hitler gained significant influence over the churches. They tried to redefine Jesus, crucified and risen, into the *übermencsh*—the mascot of the Aryan race. Today, we can see efforts to redefine Jesus, crucified and risen, into the rugged individualist entrepreneur—the mascot for capitalism.[52]

This particular Babylon focuses many on blaming the government for our problems—a very good strategy, as a weakened government will not be able to restrain powerful corporate forces. Further, when this scapegoating is seen as possibly not enough to do the trick, this Babylon shifts our focus to migrant workers and Hispanic immigrants as the root of all of our suffering.

Meanwhile, our national and world wealth continues to flow up the economic scale, with few benefits trickling down. The über-wealthy do not see (or do not admit to seeing) that if they hold all the cards, none are left to pass around.

Indeed, the über-wealthy are slaves of domination, too. Their insulation from life and death comes from becoming increasingly wealthy, even if it means that others must starve. Our human need for insulation will cause people to justify fulfilling their perceived personal needs at any cost. These modern-day kings of domination do not see that they, too, have given away their freedom in the bargain for an affirmation that starves them of any real or lasting meaning. When they—like Pharaoh, Caesar, and the rest of us—get to their deathbed, will they wonder if their plunder was worth it?

What does it say when our highest corporate value is "stockholder value," placed over stewardship of the earth and culture, treatment of workers, and the welfare of those who will come after us? What does it say when our highest individual value is the size of our retirement account?

But the über-wealthy are not the only ones participating in this winner-take-all game. Nearly all who live in denial and domination participate in the illusion. The skillful marketers hook many people into buying into their vision by promoting it as "a vision for humanity," and we consumers buy into the idea that unfettered capitalism will get us there. We cling to the American Dream, a promise that tells us we can "make it" by trading our time and lives in chase of this particular wind. Many of us cling to this promise even after our dream of enjoying ever-increasing wealth has been replaced with the nightmare of our repossessed homes.

We know that we cannot continue to live on this planet that has given home to nearly seven billion people if we continue to consume our its in the way so many of us do. Yet we believe that we cannot be happy unless we not only maintain our current "high" standard of living but also endeavor to seek a "higher" one. (Remember, this is deliberately marketed as a vision for humanity!) As a result, we feel guilty and stuck.

Yet something within us senses that any system that allows, even requires, so many to die of hunger cannot possibly be ideal. When we come to our senses, we become angry and we want things to change—now! We are tempted to think that we would have to change it all and with one great big lever. Not finding such a lever, we give up.

It is good to remember that Jesus did not succumb to the hope-defeating idea that we need a lever big enough to change all of it at once. This idea destroys our hope, invalidates our participation, and leaves us vulnerable to submission and to the dominance expressed in violence. Jesus saw that small groups of apprentices, practicing baptismal awareness in God's Reign of Mutuality, could act like seed, leaven, and light and so transform the world's illusion into God's reality a little at a time. He trusted that God would complete God's vision, and so he participated in it.

> The gifts he gave were that some would be apostles, some prophets, some evangelists, some pastors and teachers, to equip the saints for the work of ministry, for building up the body of Christ, until all of us come to the unity of the faith and of the knowledge of the Son of God, to maturity, to the measure of the full stature of Christ. (Ephesians 4:11-13)

Jesus has called the church into the deep spiritual practice of baptismal awareness and—simultaneously and inextricably—risky, public nonviolent leadership in the everyday world: participation in God's Reign of Mutuality. He called for his disciples to be apprentices, practitioners of his way in the midst of whatever kingdom of domination holds sway. He taught that the Spirit would give the gifts necessary for the community to come to the full stature of Christ: the embrace of our life-as-it-is in the Reign of God.

Restored as God's Partner-People

Many challenges face any congregation or church tradition that might seek to follow Jesus in carrying the cross of nonviolent public leadership.

We are first challenged in the fact that our traditions, practices, and expectations of the church have not prepared us for this work. We have seen the church as a place of comfort that helps individuals traverse this vale of tears more than as a community charged with the healing and appreciation of the earth.

Another challenge is situational: Given that the populace has been treated to so many differing views that bear the Christian brand, might this not appear to be just one more flavor of Christian ice cream—and a costly one at that? In the Pacific Northwest, Lutheran and other formerly mainline[53] churches are seen as a medieval jousting club might be seen: quaint, beside the point, and potentially dangerous.

However, we also seem to be in one of those periodic windows of opportunity during which people may be open to Jesus' call to follow him and lead one another in carrying our cross. Many North Americans have called out the blatant abuse of power exercised in the U.S. invasion of Iraq. Moreover, many have seen the U.S. doctrine of rapid dominance not only fail to meet its military goals but also fail to win the hearts and minds of both those against whom it has been carried out and those for whom it has supposedly been employed.

Many Americans are vocalizing their frustration about participating in the domination of "just another empire" as well as their grief at no longer being able to affirm a culture that appears to no longer affirm them. People in North America and around the world are rejecting that anything can possibly justify a century of genocide, torture of prisoners, fear tactics used to sway public opinion, and the underlying capacity of good people to do terrible things for either personal gain or at the command of authorities. Many are saying that a culture trending toward a multinational corporate hegemony, always on the lookout for cheaper raw materials and lower-cost workers, is just not working for the human race. Many are realizing that exploiting the "capital" of natural resources as if they were infinite for the sake of realizing short-term profit makes no long-term sense. Many are realizing that dumping industrial waste into the environment as if that produced no ill effect wounds us all.

While many will point fingers only at corporate greed, bad government, the media, or religion, the real culprit is far more frightening. Each of us is capable of being a Hitler or one of the millions who passively accepted his rule, because each of us is vulnerable to harboring a desperate need for the affirmation of culture and the need to affirm culture. Any one of us could participate in torture or deny that it is happening. We all carry the possibility of Auschwitz inside us and could express that potential in new ways that are not easily recognizable when our eyes are blinded by the shadow of our fear.[54]

We all participate in the culture of domination. We can begin, however incomplete such a beginning might be, to consciously withdraw our support from it.

Our participation in domination culture does not mean that human beings are totally depraved, nor does it mean that the creation is a hellhole. It means that we are vulnerable yet often reject our vulnerability as something that would prevent us from enjoying a good life.

Fortunately, it does not end here. We can practice embrace of life-as-it-is and find that our very specific daily existence is affirmed by that which is beyond us. We are called by the Creator of All to participate in the restoration of the shalom society, in the inbreaking and emergence of God's Reign of Mutuality. We are called to be the Body of Christ in the world—that is, to be apprentices who do what Jesus would do if he were us.

Despite opinion to the contrary the Christian movement can once again sit at the feet of Jesus and learn to be more fully human and develop a more authentic human community. Jesus can teach us that to be human is to embrace our power and our vulnerability, our life and our death. He can teach us that in so doing we become capable of living in mutuality with one another and with a fragile planet that is in our care, even as we in its care. Jesus can teach us to, while living in the midst of a culture of denial and domination, wholeheartedly follow him in nonviolent cultural change and accept the potential costs. Jesus can teach us to accept these risks not because we have either a death wish or a superiority complex, but because the Creator of the Universe has risked all to restore the earth. We cannot help but joyfully respond to God's Reign of Mutuality; we are captivated by its very beauty.

As the Psalmist wrote:

> *O Lord, our Sovereign,*
> *how majestic is your name in all the earth!*
> *You have set your glory above the heavens.*
> *Out of the mouths of babes and infants*
> *you have founded a bulwark because of your foes,*
> *to silence the enemy and the avenger.*
> *When I look at your heavens,*
> *the work of your fingers,*
> *the moon and the stars that you have established;*
> *what are human beings that you are mindful of them,*
> *mortals that you care for them?*
> *Yet you have made them a little lower than God,*

and crowned them with glory and honor.
You have given them dominion over
the works of your hands;
you have put all things under their feet,
all sheep and oxen,
and also the beasts of the field,
the birds of the air, and the fish of the sea,
whatever passes along the paths of the seas.
O Lord, our Sovereign,
how majestic is your name in all the earth! (Psalm 8)

Jesus understood the influence of culture and how domination culture deforms human beings and human community. He called his apprentices to engage in deep spiritual work of baptismal awareness so that they might become free enough to differentiate themselves from the domination culture around them. In this freedom, they could accept his call to nonviolent leadership within domination culture.

Jesus continues to call us, his apprentices, to take up our cross and follow him. This calling, however, is not just some plan by God to get some work out of us. As Psalm 8 says so well, God heals us by restoring us to our true identity as God's partner-people.

We alone do not make God's Reign of Mutuality come. God does. We hope and pray, "Thy kingdom come." Having been called by Jesus to apprenticeship, we are given new freedom to explore the possibilities within that reign. We pray that we might be salt, leaven, and light as we participate now in God's kingdom now, and yet to come.

AFTERWORD

Endless Possibilities

We are left with a question: How could baptismal awareness and nonviolent public leadership in the emerging Reign of God's Mutuality be lived out in community?

The possibilities are endless, each depending on the context and God's calling in the midst of that context. Because the God beyond our idea of God affirms us, we are free to imagine living out love. Because we are affirmed by God, we are free to imagine participating in God's reign without having to imagine ourselves as being perfect. Because God affirms us, we are free to be traditional in a vibrant way and/or to do things that are very different and even shocking.

Many are longing for a response to the deep challenges facing the human race and see possibilities within the life and teaching of Jesus. Both those on the inner and outer edges of the institutional church have felt their baptismal ministry and calling to be muted or even impossible within the current missional imagination and structures of the church.

Often, congregations seem more interested in their own survival than in the restoration of the earth. Many of the efforts toward revitalizing congregations have been focused on finding technical answers to a deeply challenging, adaptive problem. The key issue is theological and contextual: What is the church called to do and be, and how could that be lived out in a particular context at this time?

I have a vision for one way to live out this freedom in community. I call it the Catacomb churches: Resisting Empire, Restoring Creation, Being Human. The Catacomb churches will be a community of house churches practicing baptismal awareness and participation in God's Reign of Mutuality. Each house church will meet weekly for community, food, fun, word, sacrament, silence, personal prayer, and for plotting participation in God's Reign of Mutuality through public nonviolent leadership.

Participants and leaders having some or all of these characteristics will be sought from the larger community:

- Restless about the way things are
- Have already shown leadership
- Possess a sense of humor and playfulness
- Hold a deep commitment to the creation
- Willing to try something new and stick with it
- Looking for a community of mutual support for deep inner work and engagement with the larger world

Some of these might be members of current churches. So that the church in its current form would not be invalidated, we would encourage healthy conversation with pastoral staff of those churches and continued participation, even partnership, in ministry.

Full participation in the Catacomb churches will require a high level of commitment. Each full participant and leader will continually participate in and practice a multi-year catechetical and leadership development process. This process will be based on ancient forms as well as the ancient church's understanding that baptism into the church requires a significant change in basic allegiance and worldview. Some of this will take place in the house church; some will take place within the larger body of Catacomb churches.

I envision each house church having two leaders. Both will be selected carefully and formed in this multi-year catechetical and leadership development process. In their leadership roles, the house church leaders will have ongoing supervision and support.

The Catacomb churches will develop a rule of life and review it from time to time. The purpose for a rule of life is to provide people with a way to examine and, as appropriate, modify their life choices toward enhancing both enjoyment of life and appreciation of their life-supportive role in serving others and the earth. Participants in the decision-making processes of a house church will be required to tithe, participate in their house church and the larger Catacomb community, engage in personal prayer, reduce their carbon footprint, and so on.

This rule of life will take into consideration the questions facing the human race:

- How do we understand and manage life and death as human beings?
- How do we live together despite our significant differences of worldview and culture?
- How will we live on this planet in a way that respects the ecosystem and those who will live after us?

The house churches will come together about once a month and during certain liturgical seasons for corporate worship. They will gather at borrowed or rented facilities.

The Catacomb churches will be a joint mission of Lutherans and Episcopalians, as each tradition brings unique gifts to the table. Moreover, the fact that these denominations are working together on many projects and are learning from each other is a sign of the deep reformation that is taking place in our time.

A tendency of many churches is to become cults of personality. This is the opposite of mutuality! The hope for the Catacomb churches is that, with the oversight of two bishops and a mission pastor, they will be healthy and vibrant for many years, and that new ones will constantly be in development.

Many understand "leadership" as authoritarian—that is, as an exercise of dominance over subservient others. Jesus' understanding of leadership was to orient people to the inbreaking reign of God and to invite them to become full partners with him in that reign.

- God is committed to loving and healing the world.
- God invites our participation in that healing.
- Our participation is one way God is healing us.
- God won't stop until the healing is complete.

We are again in a time of deep reformation. The Constantinian and Modern eras are simultaneously ending. It makes sense to explore new ways in which to be church while remaining in communion with historic church bodies. As Constantine's vision of the church dies, the early church has become fertile ground for our imagination as we seek new visions. The last great reformation encouraged a way to see change as an integral part of the church's mission and life: *Ecclesia semper reformanda est.* The church must always be reforming.

Formation of the Catacomb churches is an attempt to explore reforming both the way to structure church and our imagination about what church is here to do.

Advantages of the House Church Structure

Two factors are key in support of a structure such as this.

Stewardship – House churches need fewer resources than larger, traditionally organized churches. This means that more of their resources can go into community, spiritual practices, formation, and mission. With each participating household tithing and low infrastructure cost, at least 50 percent of a house church's income will remain with that house church for use in its community life and leadership in the world. Furthermore, as we are in an age in which the larger meaning of stewardship must be recovered, we are called to live joyously within the sustainable limits of the earth's resources.

Baptismal Calling – Because there are no large infrastructure costs, there is less temptation to protect revenue by playing it safe. Each house church will have more freedom in discerning and carrying out its leadership in the world than is practicable in a large congregational model. This does not mean there will not be oversight and discipline with respect to a house church's leadership in the world, but there will be a greater range of possible forms of leadership, from service at a local assisted living center to challenging the wisdom and validity of the military industrial complex.

Holy Imagination

Challenging the idea that the church was synonymous with the institution of the Roman Catholic Church of his day, Luther said that the church is the community of believers gathered around word and sacrament. Today, we might need to amend his description: The church is the community of people, formed by word and sacrament, that practices the mutuality of baptismal awareness and participates with Jesus in nonviolent public leadership in God's Reign of Mutuality.

This would say that we are inextricably called to both deep spiritual development and participation in restoration of the world. We are called by God as a part of the deep affirmation we receive through Jesus Christ.

Endnotes

1. Christopher Browning, *Ordinary Men* (New York: Harper Perennial, 1992) 184.
2. Philip Zimbardo, *The Lucifer Effect, (*New York: Random House Trade Paperbacks, 2007) 213.
3. R. J. Rummel, *Statistics of Democide: Genocide and Mass Murder since 1900* (Charlottesville, VA: Center for National Security Law, School of Law, University of Virginia, 1997; and Transaction Publishers, Rutgers University), http://www.hawaii.edu/powerkills/notes5.htm
4. Ernest Becker, *Denial of Death* (New York: Free Press, 1973) 26-27.
5. Pyszczynski, Solomon, Greenberg, "In the Wake of 9/11": The Psychology of Terror," American PsychologicalAssociation (APA) January 2003) 46.
6. Ernest Becker, *Denial of Death* (New York: Free Press, 1973) 178.
7. René Girard, *I See Satan Fall Like Lightning,* trans. James G. Williams (Maryknoll; Orbis Books, 2001).
8. Walter Wink, *The Powers That Be: Theology for a New Millennium* (New York: Doubleday, 1998).
9. Dan Erlander, *Manna and Mercy* (Mercer Island: The Order of St. Martins and Theresa, 1992) 4.
10. Bob Altemeyer, *The Authoritarians,* http://home.cc.umanitoba.ca/~altemey/ (2006).
11. "Acceptance" is considered an acceptable antonym for denial; however, I am uncomfortable with the word's use here, as it can denote a sense of perfectionism. I think we can only practice the embrace of our vulnerability and power, not achieve it fully. But "embrance" as the act of practicing baptismal awareness is not a word, and "recognition" is too passive.
12. Rodney Stark, *The Rise of Christianity,* (New York: Harper Collins, 1997) 206.
13. Martin Luther, *Luther's Works, Vol. 31 : Career of the Reformer I,* ed. Harold J. Grimm and Helmut T. Lehmann (Philadelphia: Fortress Press, 1999, © 1957) §31:51.
14. Thomas Merton, *New Seeds of Contemplation* (New York: New Directions, 1961) 38.
15. Paul Tillich, *The Courage to Be,* 2d ed., (New Haven and London: Yale University Press, 2000) 186-190 (but read the whole book).
16. Joshua E. S. Phillips, "Unveiling Iraq's teenage prostitutes." http://dir.salon.com/story/news/feature/2005/06/24/prostitutes/index.html
17. Ursula K. Leguin, *The Earthsea Trilogy* (New York: Houghton Mifflin, 2005) 363.
18. Dietrich Bonhoeffer, *The Cost of Discipleship* (New York: Macmillan Company, 1949) 127.
19. Mahatma Gandhi et al, *The Essential Gandh*i, 2d ed, (New York: Vintage Press, 2002) 82.

20. Martin Luther, *Luther's Works, Vol. 31 : Career of the Reformer I*, ed. Harold J. Grimm and Helmut T. Lehmann (Philadelphia: Fortress Press, 1999, © 1957) §31:51.

21. Dietrich Bonhoeffer, *Letters and Papers from Prison*, ed Eberhard Bethge (New York: Collier Books, 1972) 361.

22. In their book, *Saving Paradise*, Rita Brock and Rebecca Parker make the case that focusing on the crucifixion of Jesus was used as a tool by an authoritarian expression of Christianity to increase worldview defense on the part of their subjects. They note that the art in catacombs and cathedrals before the 11th century tend to focus on Jesus as the source of new life, and baptism as entrance into the earth as paradise. At first, their thesis seems contradictory to that of this book. I am not convinced that it is. I think that Jesus is leading us to a deep engagement with life-as-it-is, which is life that includes death. As I stated earlier, when people who have not deeply engaged death are reminded of death, they tend to become more likely to protect the status quo, obey their leaders, and react more violently towards those who are different. This is the finding of Terror Management Theory. It is also a dynamic that Hermann Goering and authoritarian leaders have well understood. I believe that the baptismal awareness brought by Jesus gives us capacity to resist this dynamic, because in baptismal awareness we learn to embrace life-as-it-is and are not as dependent on culture's insulation in dealing with death.

23. Ronald Heifetz and Martin Linsky, *Leadership Without Easy Answers* (Boston: Harvard University Press, 1998).

24. Walter Brueggeman, *Biblical Perspectives on Evangelism* (Nashville: Abingdon Press, 1993) 45.

25. Dire Straits, "Brothers in Arms", *Brothers in Arms*, 1985, Warner Brothers.

26. J. K. Rowling, *Harry Potter and the Deathly Hallows* (New York: Arthur Levin Books, 2007) 720.

27. God's affirmation of life-as-it-is is does not mean that God affirms everything we do; rather, that God affirms our existence, our life. God would not affirm selling or using crystal meth, as both are ways to avoid the anxiety of life: The user numbs him or herself to life; the dealer experiences power over the user.

28. *Mythology: The Illustrated Anthology of World Myth and Storytelling, ed C. Scott Littleton* (Thunder Bay Press, 2002) 14.

29. Marcus J. Borg, N.T. Wright, *The Meaning of Jesus: Two Visions* (New York: Harper Collins, 1999) 32.

30. Marcus J. Borg, *The Heart of Christianity* (San Francisco:Harper SanFrancisco, 1989) 130.

31. K. C. Hanson, "The Galilean Fishing Economy and the Jesus Tradition," *Biblical Theology Bulletin* 27 (1997) 99-111.

32. Richard Rohrbaugh, Presentation to the Byberg Preaching Workshop, http://byberg-preaching.org/blog/media-archive/byberg-2010/

33. N.T. Wright, *The New Testament and the People of God* (San Francisco: HarperSanFrancisco, 1992) 244-338.

34. Marcus J. Borg, John Dominic Crossan, *The Last Week: What the Gospels Really Teach about Jesus' Final Days in Jerusalem* (New York: HarperOne, 2007).

35. Martin Luther King, "Nonviolence: The Only Road to Freedom," *A Testament of Hope: The Essential Writings of Martin Luther King* (San Francisco: HarperSanFrancisco, 1991) 59.

36. Ibid., 19.
37. Dietrich Bonhoeffer, *The Cost of Discipleship* (New York: Macmillan Company, 1949) 127.
38. Mahatma Gandhi et al, *The Essential Gandhi*, 2d ed, (New York: Vintage Press, 2002), 90.
39. Murray Bowen, "Family Projection Process," http://www.thebowencenter.org/pages/conceptfpp.html
40. I have learned much from C. S. Lewis, but his ideas surrounding the "deep magic" requirement of Aslan's death is confusing to many and in some ways supports the notion of a cosmic need for violence.
41. Douglas John Hall, *Thinking the Faith, Professing the Faith, Confessing the Faith* (Minneapolis: Fortress Press, 1989, 1991, 1993). See especially "Confessing the Faith," 200-340.
42. Martin Luther King, "I Have a Dream," speech delivered from the steps of the Lincoln Memorial, Washington, DC, August 28, 1963.
43. Rita Nakashima Brock, Rebecca Ann Parker, *Saving Paradise* (Boston: Beacon Press, 2008) 115.
44. Marian Hostetler, *They Loved Their Enemies* (Scottsdale, PA: Herald Press) 16.
45. Ibid., 18.
46. Dietrich Bonhoeffer, *The Cost of Discipleship*, (New York: Macmillan Company, 1949) 102.
47. Douglas John Hall, *The Cross in Our Context* (Minneapolis: Augsburg Fortress, 2003) 1.
48. Martin Luther King Jr." Letter from Birmingham City Jail, open letter, April 16, 1963.
49. Karl Barth, "Faith as Confession," Chapter 4 in *Dogmatics in Outline*, trans. G. T. Thompson (New York: Harper & Bros., 1959).
50. Dietrich Bonhoeffer, *The Cost of Discipleship* (New York: Macmillan Company, 1949) 35.
51. Douglas John Hall, *Confessing the Faith* (Minneapolis: Fortress Press, 1993) 467.
52. This is a quote from my friend, Andy Rutrough.
53. "Mainline" churches, while a useful term for identifying many moderate to liberal churches, have declined enough to prefix the term with "formerly." Some observers have suggested that "Sideline" churches might be a more appropriate expression. I think the demise of these churches is but a preparation for another resurrection. I look forward to being a part of that.
54. Ruth Rehmann, "The Man in the Pulpit: Questions for a Father," trans. Christoph Lohmann and Pemela Hohmann (Lincoln: University of Nebraska Press, 1997)

Acknowledgements

No author writes a book on their own. We are deeply formed by our larger culture, our social location within that culture, and the many people who have loved and struggled with us. I have been formed by many people, and I bear the marks of their hands.

I want to thank the Text Study group that meets at First Lutheran in Mount Vernon, Washington, for the many good arguments we have had over the years. As I have been forming my perspective, they have challenged and affirmed my thoughts in ways that have been indispensable.

I continue to be blessed by the work of Dan Erlander, who has expressed the Good News with so much humor and love.

I thank Dick Wendt, David Greenlee, Paul Sundberg, Eileen Hanson, Larry Pennings, and Rachel Simonson for their support as a part of our collegial supervision group. There is nothing in the world like a good friends who can nail you with a hard question!

Many people helped with the later stages of writing, giving me input and asking good questions. My thanks to Kathryn Arndt, Laurin Vance, Herb Sanborn, and Red Burchfield for their reading of this book in its late stages and their excellent input that helped shape its final form.

Many thanks go to the congregations of the Komo Kulshan Cluster. I appreciate very much their willingness to engage with a pastor/priest who often pushes the edge.

I want to thank the pastoral staff of the Komo Kulshan Cluster: Vicki Wesen, Rilla Barrett, and Dennis Taylor. They have listened to my crazy ideas and questions and have helped me witness the growth of the ideas I have put forth in this book. They heard many a rough verbalization of these ideas, and their patience and insights have been a deep blessing.

Chara Curtis has put in many hours editing this book. I tend to write as if I am speaking, and Chara helps me translate my words into a form more suitable for print. I appreciate her fearless questioning of my ideas and her willingness to engage my responses.

Andy Rutrough has been my most constant conversation partner since seminary. Without him, this book would not exist.

I thank my family for giving me permission to spend long hours in writing. It has been great fun working with Lauren on the painting that graces the cover of this book and with Shelby on the cover layout and the illustration of mutuality. To my wife Sheryl, I can only say, "Thank you!"

Finally, books are their own kind of vanity, their own kind of search for significance. Any significance other than the affirmation of life by the God beyond our idea of God is straw. However, being affirmed by the One, I have dared to write such straw in order that I might learn to live in the freedom of God's love.

About the Author

Terry Kyllo attended seminary at the Lutheran School of Theology at Chicago, receiving his Masters of Divinity (a four-year degree required for Lutheran ordination) in 1991. Terry serves as a pastor of an ecumenical partnership of five churches in the Skagit Valley of Washington state. As pastor he helps imagine, support, equip, and oversee all the baptized in ministry as all participate in God's love for and healing of the world.

Terry grew up in Lacrosse, Washington, a wheat-farming town of 300 people in southeastern corner of the state. His father was a custodian at the school, and his mother was a homemaker who was diagnosed with Multiple Sclerosis when Terry was five. From the experience of his mother's illness, Terry learned that life is fragile and is to be honored. He is still learning from his father's faithfulness in the midst of illness.

Terry's path to pastoral vocation began when in high school he was told that he could not accept evolutionary theory and be a Christian. This created a tension in his life between Christianity and the modern world that led him away from Christianity for a time. Eventually realizing that it must be possible to both be a Christian and live in today's world, he engaged in conversation and study to discover the underlying bases for these seemingly contradictory viewpoints and to reconcile those ideas. *Apprenticeship* is his second book, following *Being Human: The Image of the Service God*.

Terry lives in Anacortes, Washington, with his wife and their two children.